Totally Teabreads

Totally Teabreads

Barbara Albright and
Leslie Weiner

• • •

Illustrations by Diana Thewlis

ST. MARTIN'S PRESS ◆ NEW YORK

Cover photograph by Michael Weiss
Cover china—Petite Fleur by Villeroy & Boch
Cover teabread—Toasted Almond Apricot Loaf
(recipe on page 73)

Library of Congress Cataloging-in-Publication Data

Albright, Barbara.
    Totally teabreads / Barbara Albright and Leslie Weiner.
        p.   cm.
    ISBN 0-312-10561-4 (pbk.)
    1. Bread.   I. Weiner, Leslie.   II. Title.
    TX769.A4853 1994   2. Cookery.
    641.8′15—dc20
                                                                    93-43659
                                                                    CIP

First edition: March 1994
10   9   8   7   6   5   4   3   2   1

*To Barbara Anderson, our editor, for giving us a very long time
to finish this book.*

*To Samantha and Lauren, our toddlers, who are the reason this book
took so long to do.*

*To Ted and Lowell, our husbands, who have consumed more than their fair
share of baked goods—both good and bad.*

Contents

Metric and Imperial Conversions

All the recipes in *Totally Teabreads* were tested using U.S. Customary measuring cups and spoons. Following are approximate conversions for weight and metric measurements. Results may vary slightly when using approximate conversions. Ingredients also vary from country to country. However, we wanted to include this list so you'll be able to make teabreads wherever you may be.

• VOLUME CONVERSIONS •

U.S. Customary	Approximate Metric Conversion (ml)
⅛ teaspoon	0.5 ml
¼ teaspoon	1.0 ml
½ teaspoon	2.5 ml
1 teaspoon	5.0 ml
1 tablespoon (3 teaspoons)	15.0 ml
2 tablespoons	30.0 ml
3 tablespoons	45.0 ml
¼ cup (4 tablespoons)	60.0 ml
⅓ cup (5⅓ tablespoons)	79.0 ml
½ cup (8 tablespoons)	118.0 ml
⅔ cup (10⅔ tablespoons)	158.0 ml
¾ cup (12 tablespoons)	177.0 ml
1 cup	237.0 ml

• LENGTH CONVERSIONS •

U.S. Inches	*Approximate Metric Conversion (cm)*
⅜ inch	Scant 1 cm
½ inch	1.0 cm
⅝ inch	1.5 cm
1 inch	2.5 cm
2 inches	5.0 cm
3 inches	7.5 cm
4 inches	10.0 cm
5 inches	12.5 cm
6 inches	15.0 cm
7 inches	17.5 cm
8 inches	20.0 cm
9 inches	22.5 cm
10 inches	25.0 cm
11 inches	27.5 cm
12 inches	30.0 cm
13 inches	32.5 cm
14 inches	35.0 cm
15 inches	37.5 cm

· COMMONLY USED INGREDIENT CONVERSIONS ·

ALL-PURPOSE FLOUR, UNSIFTED AND SPOONED INTO THE CUP

Volume	Ounces	Grams
¼ cup	1.1 oz	31 gm
⅓ cup	1.5 oz	42 gm
½ cup	2.2 oz	63 gm
1 cup	4.4 oz	125 gm

GRANULATED SUGAR

Volume	Ounces	Grams
1 teaspoon	.1 oz	4 gm
1 tablespoon	.4 oz	12 gm
¼ cup	1.8 oz	50 gm
⅓ cup	2.4 oz	67 gm
½ cup	3.5 oz	100 gm
1 cup	7.1 oz	200 gm

FIRMLY PACKED BROWN SUGAR

Volume	Ounces	Grams
1 tablespoon	.5 oz	14 gm
¼ cup	1.9 oz	55 gm
⅓ cup	2.6 oz	73 gm
½ cup	3.9 oz	110 gm
1 cup	7.8 oz	220 gm

UNSALTED BUTTER

Volume	Ounces	Grams
1 tablespoon	.5 oz	14 gm
¼ cup	2.0 oz	57 gm
⅓ cup	2.6 oz	76 gm
½ cup	4.0 oz	113 gm
1 cup	8.0 oz	127 gm

NUTS

Volume	Ounces	Grams
¼ cup	1.0 oz	28 gm
⅓ cup	1.3 oz	38 gm
½ cup	2.0 oz	57 gm
1 cup	4.0 oz	113 gm

◆ OVEN TEMPERATURE CONVERSIONS ◆

Fahrenheit	Approximate Celsius (Centigrade)
300°	150°
325°	160°
350°	175°
375°	190°
400°	200°
425°	220°
450°	230°

Totally Teabreads

Introduction

Originally "in our alliterative style," we wanted to call this book "Quintessentially Quickbreads," but we didn't think that would fit on the cover of this book. *Totally Teabreads* seems to fill the bill (and the cover). By teabreads (or quick breads), we mean breads that are made without yeast. Instead, these breads are leavened with baking powder, baking soda, and eggs. They are considerably faster to prepare than yeast breads and don't require kneading.

Teabreads come in all shapes and sizes—especially in our book! Even though we have called them breads, many people, including our toddlers, Samantha and Lauren, were not fooled. It was cake to them. You might feel the same way that they do.

The book is divided into several sections with breads and spreads for any time of day. Some of the breads are light and airy; others are hearty and dense. The ingredients used in the bread will greatly affect the final volume and texture. For example, cheese creates some tunneling. Oats give breads a somewhat dense and chewy texture. Not surprisingly, the "Somewhat Healthier Teabreads" are slightly less tender because they have less fat and no egg yolks. To keep these breads as flavorful as possible, we included sugar and a small amount of salt. Sugar helps to keep the breads tender. The breads will taste flat if you omit the salt.

We have carefully developed every single recipe in the book—some of the recipes were tested more times than we ever imagined would be necessary or possible. With all of these tests, many people want to know what we do with the breads that we've baked. We have found that we tend to eat more of breads that need more work. As we nibble away on the bread, we try to figure out what went wrong. We also send the breads, including rejects, to work with our husbands, and we are grateful to our guinea pigs at Horizon Textiles, Anaheim Mills, and Shering-Plough International for their consumption of endless quantities of teabreads.

Making Perfect Teabreads

BAKING

Before preparing the teabreads, read each recipe carefully, assemble the equipment, prepare the pan (for best results, use good-quality metal baking pans), and measure the ingredients. This simple procedure (which holds true for all recipes) will help avoid many mishaps.

Preheat the oven to the specified temperature and check the temperature of your oven with an oven thermometer. (Mercury oven thermometers work best.) Oven temperatures vary, however, so check the breads at the minimum baking time recommended in each recipe to avoid overbaking, especially when trying the recipes for the first time. Bake the bread on the middle oven rack. Test for doneness as directed in the recipe. Most of the breads will be golden brown. Breads with less sugar (savory breads) brown less.

Follow the recipe directions for cooling the breads. This usually includes a short cooling period in the baking pan on a wire rack to firm up the bread slightly before removing it to a wire rack to cool completely. If necessary, run a knife around the edges of the bread to loosen the sides from the pan. Cooling the bread on a wire rack with adequate air circulation will help prevent it from becoming soggy. For square or round loaves, serve the bread from the pan, or invert onto a wire rack or baking sheet. Invert again onto wire rack to cool. Use a serrated knife to cut the breads.

We do not live in a standardized world, and pan sizes are no exception. Try to stay within ¼ inch of each specified pan dimension for the best results. For example, you can use a pan labeled "9¼ × 5¼ × 2¾ inch" in recipes that specify "9 × 5 × 3 inch."

MEASURING

Be sure to use the appropriate measuring cups for dry and liquid ingredients. Use measuring spoons instead of flatware. Level off measuring spoons and dry measuring cups with the flat edge of a spatula. Read measurements for liquid ingredients at eye level. (Refer to individual ingredients for specific measuring instructions.)

STORAGE

Teabreads are best served shortly after they are baked, but many can be stored successfully. Be sure to cool the breads completely before storing them in an airtight container. Breads made with perishable items (such as cheese and meat) should be refrigerated, especially in warm weather. It's not a bad idea to refrigerate all breads if the weather is very hot.

To reheat refrigerated bread, toast slices for about 2 minutes in a toaster oven. Pieces of the bread can also be reheated by wrapping them in foil and baking in a 350°F. oven for 5 to 10 minutes.

To store breads in the freezer for up to one month, wrap completely cooled breads in plastic wrap and then in aluminum foil. Store in an airtight container for the best results. Be sure to label and date the bread before freezing so that you do not have any mystery packages in your freezer.

INGREDIENTS

FLOUR

Unless otherwise specified, the recipes call for all-purpose flour, as this is the type of flour that most people have on hand. To measure any type of flour, lightly spoon the flour into the appropriate dry measuring cup. Try not to be heavy-handed. Level it off with the straight edge of a knife. Do not tap the cup or dip it into the flour or you will end up with more flour than is needed.

SUGAR

We've used granulated sugar, confectioners' sugar, and brown sugar in these recipes. In addition to adding sweetness, sugar is important to the texture of baked items. In our recipes we have used enough sugar to make good-tasting, tender breads, but they are not excessively sweet. Measure granulated sugar by filling the appropriate dry measuring cup. Level it off with the straight edge of a knife. Measure confectioners' sugar in the same way that you measure flour. Light and dark brown sugar are basically interchangeable in recipes. Dark brown sugar will produce darker breads. To measure brown sugar, press it firmly into the appropriate-size dry measuring cup(s) until it is level with the top edge. It should hold the form of the cup when turned out.

Store brown sugar in airtight containers in a cool place. One manufacturer recommends freezing brown sugar for lengthy storage, and most manufacturers include softening directions on the package should your brown sugar become dry and rocklike. One recommended method is to place the brown sugar in an airtight plastic container, cover the surface of the sugar with a piece of plastic wrap, and top with a folded moist paper towel. Seal the container for eight to twelve hours before removing the towel.

Whether you've had to soften your brown sugar or not, we've found that it is a good idea to squeeze the brown sugar between your fingertips as you add it to the mixture to eliminate sugar clumps in the finished product.

BAKING POWDER AND BAKING SODA

These two items are not interchangeable. Use whichever is called for in the recipe. Use double-acting baking powder, which is the type most readily available. (We have noticed that a few single-acting baking powders have been sneaking onto grocers' shelves.)

Double-acting baking powder enables leavening to occur both at room temperature and during baking. It contains two acid components, calcium acid phosphate and sodium aluminum sulfate, along with an alkali component, sodium bicarbonate (baking soda), and cornstarch. Adding liquid to baking powder causes a chemical reaction between the acid and alkali, forming carbon dioxide and water. Leavening occurs when heat causes carbon dioxide gas to be released into the dough.

When acid ingredients (such as buttermilk, yogurt, sour cream, citrus, cranberries, and molasses) are used in baking, it is usually necessary to add baking soda (sodium bicarbonate—an alkali) to balance the acid-alkali ratio.

Make sure your baking powder and baking soda are fresh. They can lose their potency if stored past the expiration date or if moisture gets into the container.

SALT

Our recipes use very little salt and, when divided among servings, the amount of salt is minimal. Don't leave it out. We think you will find that just a little bit greatly enhances the flavor of most baked goods.

EGGS

Select large, uncracked eggs. Letting the eggs reach room temperature before use makes it easier to incorporate them into the batter, but do not let them stand at room temperature for more than two hours. Because of the potential danger of salmonella in raw eggs, it is not advisable to taste any mixture containing uncooked eggs.

To bring eggs to room temperature in a hurry, submerge them in a bowl of very warm water.

BUTTER

Use unsalted (often called sweet) butter in these bread recipes so that you can more accurately control the amount of salt in the recipe. The breads will taste better, too. Salt acts as a preservative and may mask the flavor of butter that is past its prime. Unsalted butter has a shorter shelf life, so if you are keeping it for long periods of time, be sure to freeze it. You may substitute unsalted margarine. However, do not substitute vegetable oil and expect to get the same results.

VANILLA EXTRACT

Use the real thing for better-tasting breads. Vanilla adds a full, rich flavor to most breads and it often allows you to get by with a little less sugar.

SPICES

Store spices in airtight containers away from light and heat. Older spices may lose their potency, so it is a good idea to date your containers at the time of purchase.

FRUITS

Use the fruits called for in each recipe. For example, do not substitute chopped fresh fruit for dried fruit, and vice versa.

Peanut Butter

Use commercially prepared peanut butter in our recipes. The health-food-store variety may change the texture of the baked bread.

Nuts

It is a good idea to taste nuts before using them, as they can become rancid and spoil your breads. Store nuts in airtight containers in the refrigerator or freezer. We like nuts and have used them in many recipes. If chopped nuts are supposed to be stirred into the bread batter, you can usually leave them out if you do not care for nuts. Remember, however, that the volume will decrease if you omit the nuts.

Chocolate

It is important to use the type of chocolate that is specified in each recipe. However, you can usually safely substitute equal amounts of different types of chocolate chunks or chips that are stirred into the bread batter.

Unsweetened Cocoa Powder

There are basically two types of unsweetened cocoa powder—alkalized and nonalkalized. The former has been treated with an alkali to make it less acidic. It is often called "Dutch-processed" or "European-style." In our recipes we've used nonalkalized cocoa powder because we think it gives a richer, more robust chocolate flavor to baked items, and it is readily available. (Hershey's brown container of classic cocoa powder and Nestlé's are both nonalkalized.) Measure cocoa powder the same way that you measure flour.

MAIL ORDER SOURCES

Dried Cherries
American Spoon Foods, Inc.
1668 Clarion Avenue
P.O. Box 566
Petoskey, MI 49770-0566
(616) 347-9030 or (800) 222-5886

Amon Orchards
7404 US 31 North
P.O. Box 1551
Traverse City, MI 49685
(616) 938-9160

Hazelnuts
Evonuk Oregon Hazelnuts
P.O. Box 7121
Eugene, OR 97401

Baking Equipment
Maid of Scandinavia
3244 Raleigh Avenue
Minneapolis, MN 55416
(800) 328-6722

Sweet Teabreads

• ANADAMA CORN BREAD •

Legend has it that a New England fisherman with a lazy wife, named Anna, did all the cooking and baking for his family. He created a corn and molasses yeast bread in "honor" of his wife and called it "Anna, damn her."

We combined our quick bread version of Anadama bread with traditional corn bread to create a two-toned loaf.

1 cup all-purpose flour
¾ cup yellow cornmeal
3 tablespoons granulated sugar
2 teaspoons baking powder
½ teaspoon salt

¾ cup milk, at room temperature
⅓ cup vegetable oil
2 large eggs (at room temperature), lightly beaten
2 tablespoons molasses

1. Preheat oven to 400°F. Butter an 8-inch-square baking pan. Lightly dust pan with additional flour and tap out excess.

2. In a large bowl, stir together flour, cornmeal, sugar, baking powder, and salt. In another bowl, stir together milk, oil, and eggs until blended. Make a well in center of flour mixture; add milk mixture and stir just to combine. Pour 1¼ cups of the batter into a liquid measuring cup. Stir molasses into remaining batter in bowl.

3. Pour ¾ cup of the cornmeal batter into prepared pan. Use a metal spatula to spread batter to an even layer. Pour molasses batter into pan. Use a clean metal spatula to spread batter to an even layer. Pour remaining cornmeal batter over molasses batter to form 3 cornmeal stripes.

4. *To form a feathered design:* Using the tip of a knife or skewer, draw the

tip through the surface of the batter across the stripes. Continue the process by reversing direction and pulling the tip through batter again, at ¾–inch parallel intervals. Continue until entire surface is covered.

5. Bake for 20 to 30 minutes, or until a cake tester inserted in center of bread comes out clean.

6. Remove pan to a wire rack. Cool for 10 minutes before removing bread from pan; finish cooling on rack. Store completely cooled bread in an airtight container at cool room temperature.

This bread freezes well.

Makes 12 servings

For a lower fat and cholesterol version: Use 1 cup skim milk instead of ¾ cup whole milk, reduce oil to 2 tablespoons, and substitute 2 egg whites for whole eggs. In addition, salt may be reduced to ¼ teaspoon, if desired. (The following nutrition information is based on the lower amount of salt.)

Nutrition information for lower fat, cholesterol, and sodium version per serving:

117	calories
20	grams carbohydrate
3	grams protein
3	grams fat
Trace	cholesterol
117	milligrams sodium

• BANANA CHOCOLATE CHIP LOAF •

This is a rich dessert bread that's also great for quick snacks.

1¾ cups all-purpose flour
1 teaspoon baking powder
½ teaspoon baking soda
½ teaspoon salt
⅓ cup unsalted butter, at room temperature
½ cup granulated sugar

2 large eggs, at room temperature
1 cup mashed ripe bananas (about 2 large bananas)
2 tablespoons milk
1 teaspoon vanilla extract
⅔ cup miniature semisweet chocolate chips

1. Preheat oven to 350°F. Butter a 9 × 5 × 3–inch loaf pan. Lightly dust pan with additional flour and tap out excess.

2. In a large bowl, stir together flour, baking powder, baking soda, and salt. In another bowl, and using a wooden spoon, cream together butter and sugar until blended. One at a time, add eggs, beating well with a fork after each addition. Stir in bananas, milk, and vanilla until combined. Stir in flour mixture just until blended. Stir in chips.

3. Scrape batter into prepared pan and spread evenly. Bake for 45 to 55 minutes, or until a cake tester inserted in center of bread comes out clean.

4. Remove pan to a wire rack. Cool for 10 minutes before removing bread from pan; finish cooling on rack. Store completely cooled bread in an airtight container at cool room temperature.

Makes 1 loaf; 12 to 16 slices

• BANANA PRALINE BREAD •

Praline adds crunch to this tasty loaf. It's delicious spread with a thin layer of cream cheese.

PRALINE

⅓ cup granulated sugar
3 tablespoons water

⅔ cup pecans

BREAD

1½ cups all-purpose flour
½ cup packed light brown sugar
1 teaspoon baking powder
½ teaspoon baking soda
½ teaspoon salt
1 cup mashed ripe bananas (about 2 large bananas)

2 large eggs (at room temperature), lightly beaten
⅓ cup unsalted butter, melted and cooled
2 tablespoons milk
2 teaspoons vanilla extract

1. *To prepare praline:* Lightly oil a 10-inch-diameter circle on a baking sheet. In a small, heavy saucepan, stir together granulated sugar and water. Cook over medium heat, stirring constantly, until sugar dissolves. Increase heat to high and bring mixture to a boil. Cook without stirring for 3½ minutes, or until mixture turns amber and caramelizes. Immediately add pecans and stir to coat nuts with syrup. Immediately scrape mixture onto oiled part of

prepared baking sheet. Cool for 20 minutes, or until hardened. Transfer mixture to a cutting board and chop praline.

2. *To prepare bread:* Preheat oven to 350°F. Butter an 8½ × 4½ × 2¾–inch loaf pan. Lightly dust with additional flour and tap out excess.

3. In a large bowl, stir together flour, brown sugar, baking powder, baking soda, and salt. In another bowl, stir together bananas, eggs, butter, milk, and vanilla until blended. Make a well in center of flour mixture; add banana mixture and stir just to combine. Stir in chopped praline.

4. Scrape batter into prepared pan and spread evenly. Bake for 55 to 65 minutes, or until a cake tester inserted in center of bread comes out clean.

5. Remove pan to a wire rack. Cool for 10 minutes before removing bread from pan; finish cooling on rack. Store completely cooled bread in an airtight container at cool room temperature.

Makes 1 loaf; 10 to 14 slices

• BLUEBERRY ALMOND BREAD •

Almond paste adds an inspired twist to the traditional blueberry quick bread.

2 cups all-purpose flour
2½ teaspoons baking powder
½ teaspoon salt
¾ cup granulated sugar
⅓ cup unsalted butter, at room temperature
3½ ounces (half of 7-ounce package) almond paste (at room temperature), cut into small pieces

2 large eggs, at room temperature
⅓ cup milk, at room temperature
1 teaspoon vanilla extract
⅛ teaspoon almond extract
2 cups fresh or drained, thawed frozen blueberries

1. Preheat oven to 350°F. Butter a 9 × 5 × 3–inch loaf pan. Lightly dust with additional flour and tap out excess.

2. In a small bowl, stir together flour, baking powder, and salt. In a large bowl, and using a hand-held electric mixer, cream together sugar and butter until blended. With mixer set on low, gradually beat in almond paste until combined. Increase speed to high and beat for 1 minute longer. One at a time, add eggs, beating well after each addition.

3. Stir vanilla and almond extracts into milk. In three additions each, alternately beat in flour mixture and milk mixture, beating just until combined. Stir in blueberries. Scrape batter into prepared pan and spread evenly. Bake for 55 to 65 minutes, or until a cake tester inserted in center of bread comes out clean.

4. Remove pan to a wire rack. Cool for 10 minutes before removing bread from pan; finish cooling on rack. Store completely cooled bread in an airtight container in refrigerator. Allow bread to reach room temperature before serving.

Makes 1 loaf; 12 to 16 slices

• CALIFORNIA-STYLE QUICK BREAD •

Even if it is snowing outside, you can bring a little sunshine into your life by serving this delicious bread that is packed with nuts and dried fruits from the Golden State.

2 cups all-purpose flour
2/3 cup granulated sugar
1 1/2 teaspoons baking powder
1/2 teaspoon baking soda
1/2 teaspoon salt
1/3 cup chopped dried apricots
1/3 cup raisins
1/3 cup unsalted pistachios
1/3 cup chopped walnuts

1/3 cup chopped almonds
1 cup plain low-fat yogurt, at room temperature
1/2 cup unsalted butter, melted and cooled
1 large egg (at room temperature), lightly beaten
1 1/2 teaspoons vanilla extract
1/4 teaspoon grated lemon peel

1. Preheat oven to 350°F. Butter a 9 × 5 × 3–inch loaf pan.

2. In a large bowl, stir together all but 2 tablespoons of the flour, plus the sugar, baking powder, baking soda, and salt. In another bowl, combine apricots, raisins, pistachios, walnuts, and almonds with remaining 2 tablespoons of flour. (This keeps dried fruits and nuts from sinking to bottom of bread.) In another bowl, stir together yogurt, butter, egg, vanilla, and lemon peel until blended. Make a well in center of flour mixture; add yogurt mixture and stir just to combine. Stir in dried fruit and nut mixture.

3. Scrape batter into prepared pan and spread evenly. Bake for 55 to 65 minutes, or until a cake tester inserted in center of bread comes out clean.

4. Remove pan to a wire rack. Cool for 10 minutes before removing bread from pan; finish cooling on rack. Store completely cooled bread in an airtight container at cool room temperature.

This bread freezes well.

Makes 1 loaf; 12 to 16 slices

• CANDY BAR QUICK BREAD •

We tested this bread with chopped-up Snickers, Reese's Peanut Butter Cups, and Hershey's Kisses. Don't be afraid to experiment with some of your own favorites! You can combine different bars in the same loaf if you can't make up your mind. It's a great way to use up leftover Halloween candy.

2 cups all-purpose flour
2/3 cup granulated sugar
2 teaspoons baking powder
1/2 teaspoon salt
1 1/2 cups of chocolate candy bar
   that has been chopped into
   1/2-inch pieces

3/4 cup milk, at room temperature
1/3 cup unsalted butter, melted and
   cooled
1 large egg (at room temperature),
   lightly beaten
1 1/2 teaspoons vanilla extract

1. Preheat oven to 350°F. Butter an 8 1/2 × 4 1/2 × 2 3/4-inch loaf pan.
2. In a large bowl, stir together all but 2 tablespoons of flour, plus the sugar, baking powder, and salt. In another bowl, stir together chocolate pieces and remaining 2 tablespoons of flour. (This keeps candy pieces from sinking to bottom of the bread.) In a small bowl, stir together milk, butter, egg, and vanilla until blended. Make a well in center of flour mixture; add milk mixture and stir just to combine. Stir in pieces of chocolate.
3. Scrape batter into prepared pan and spread evenly. Bake for 60 to 70 minutes, or until a cake tester inserted in center of bread comes out clean.
4. Remove pan to a wire rack. Cool for 10 minutes before removing bread from pan; finish cooling on rack. (You may need to loosen bread from pan

by running a knife around outside edges.) Store completely cooled bread in an airtight container at cool room temperature.

This bread freezes well.

Makes 1 loaf; 10 to 14 slices

• CHERRY CHOCOLATE CHIP BREAD •

The tart cherries and sweet chocolate create a tangy and irresistible flavor combination.

2 cups all-purpose flour
1/3 cup granulated sugar
1/3 cup firmly packed light brown sugar
2½ teaspoons baking powder
½ teaspoon salt
2/3 cup milk, at room temperature
½ cup unsalted butter, melted and cooled

2 large eggs (at room temperature), lightly beaten
1 teaspoon vanilla extract
1 cup coarsely chopped dried tart cherries (see Note)
½ cup semisweet chocolate chips
½ cup milk chocolate chips

1. Preheat oven to 350°F. Butter an 8½ × 4½ × 2¾–inch loaf pan. Lightly dust with additional flour and tap out excess.

2. In a large bowl, stir together flour, sugars, baking powder, and salt. In another bowl, stir together milk, butter, eggs, and vanilla until blended. Make a well in center of flour mixture; add milk mixture and stir just to combine. Stir in cherries and chips.

3. Scrape batter into prepared pan and spread evenly. Bake for 55 to 65 minutes, or until a cake tester inserted in center of bread comes out clean.

4. Remove pan to a wire rack. Cool for 10 minutes before removing bread from pan; finish cooling on rack. Store completely cooled bread in an airtight container at cool room temperature.

This bread freezes well.

Makes 1 loaf; 10 to 14 slices

Note: Dried cherries are often available in gourmet food stores, or can be ordered by mail (see page 10). Chopped pitted dates may be substituted for dried cherries.

• CHERRY VANILLA BREAD •

Real vanilla beans and dried tart cherries make this bread very special. (*Note:* This recipe uses vanilla-flavored oil, which requires two days' preparation time.)

⅓ cup vegetable oil
1 vanilla bean, split in half
   lengthwise
2 cups all-purpose flour
½ cup granulated sugar
1 teaspoon baking powder
1 teaspoon baking soda
½ teaspoon salt

1 container (8 ounces) low-fat vanilla
   yogurt, at room temperature
2 large eggs (at room temperature),
   lightly beaten
1 tablespoon vanilla extract
1½ cups coarsely chopped dried tart
   cherries (see Note)

1. Pour oil into a small, nonmetallic container. Scrape seeds from inside vanilla bean into oil. Add bean and cover. Let stand in the refrigerator for 2 days. Remove vanilla bean, squeezing it of all its liquid. Discard bean.

2. Preheat oven to 350°F. Butter a 9 × 5 × 3–inch loaf pan. Lightly dust pan with additional flour and tap out excess.

3. In a large bowl, stir together flour, sugar, baking powder, baking soda, and salt. In another bowl, stir together flavored oil, yogurt, eggs, and vanilla until blended. Make a well in center of flour mixture; add yogurt mixture and stir just to combine. Stir in cherries.

4. Scrape batter into prepared pan and spread evenly. Bake for 40 to 50 minutes, or until a cake tester inserted in center of bread comes out clean.

5. Remove pan to a wire rack. Cool for 10 minutes before removing bread from pan; finish cooling on rack. Store completely cooled bread in an airtight container at cool room temperature.

Makes 1 loaf; 12 to 16 slices

Note: Dried cherries are often available in gourmet food stores, or can be ordered by mail (see page 10). Chopped pitted dates may be substituted for dried cherries.

• CHOCOLATE CHOCOLATE-CHUNK BREAD •

This bread was created especially for serious chocolate lovers.

½ cup unsalted butter
2 ounces unsweetened chocolate
1¾ cups all-purpose flour
1 cup granulated sugar
1 teaspoon baking soda
½ teaspoon salt
1 cup buttermilk, at room
temperature

1 large egg, at room temperature
2 teaspoons vanilla extract
6 ounces milk chocolate, cut into
½-inch pieces
6 ounces bittersweet or semisweet
chocolate, cut into ½-inch pieces
¾ cup toasted coarsely broken walnuts
(see Note)

1. Preheat oven to 350°F. Butter a 9 × 5 × 3–inch loaf pan.

2. In a microwave-safe bowl, heat butter and unsweetened chocolate in a microwave oven on HIGH for 1 to 2 minutes, stirring halfway through cooking, until chocolate is melted. Let stand at room temperature for 10 minutes.

3. In a medium-sized bowl, stir together flour, sugar, baking soda, and salt. In another bowl, stir together butter mixture, buttermilk, egg, and vanilla, until blended. Make a well in center of flour mixture; add buttermilk mixture and stir just to combine. Stir in chocolate pieces and walnuts.

4. Scrape batter into prepared pan and spread evenly. Bake for 65 to 75 minutes, or until bread springs back when lightly touched in center.

5. Remove pan to a wire rack. Cool for 10 minutes before removing bread

from pan; finish cooling on rack. Store completely cooled bread in an airtight container at cool room temperature.

This bread freezes well.

Makes 1 loaf; 12 to 16 slices

Note: Place walnuts in a single layer on a baking sheet and bake at 350°F. for 5 to 7 minutes, shaking sheet a couple of times.

• CHOCOLATE-CHUNK HAZELNUT TEABREAD •

Chocolate and hazelnuts (also called filberts) are a classic European combo. Serve this sweet, rich bread after dinner with cups of steaming espresso or coffee.

2 cups all-purpose flour
¾ cup granulated sugar
2 teaspoons baking powder
½ teaspoon salt
⅔ cup milk, at room temperature
½ cup unsalted butter, melted and cooled

2 large eggs (at room temperature), lightly beaten
2 teaspoons vanilla extract
6 ounces dark chocolate (such as a Dove chocolate bar), cut into ½-inch pieces
¾ cup chopped hazelnuts (toasted, if desired; see Note)

1. Preheat oven to 350°F. Butter an 8½ × 4½ × 2¾–inch loaf pan.

2. In a medium-sized bowl, stir together flour, sugar, baking powder, and salt. In a medium-sized bowl, stir together milk, butter, eggs, and vanilla until blended. Make a well in center of flour mixture; add milk mixture and stir just to combine. Stir in chocolate and hazelnuts.

3. Scrape batter into prepared pan and spread evenly. Bake for 60 to 70 minutes, or until bread springs back when lightly touched in center.

4. Remove pan to a wire rack. Cool for 10 minutes before removing bread from pan; finish cooling on rack. Store completely cooled bread in an airtight container at cool room temperature.

This bread freezes well.

Makes 1 loaf; 10 to 14 slices

Note: To toast and skin hazelnuts, spread them in a single layer in a jelly-roll pan or on a baking sheet. Bake for 10 to 15 minutes, or until nuts are lightly browned under their skins. Wrap nuts in a clean kitchen towel and cool completely. Place nuts in a sieve and rub them against sieve to remove their skins.

• CHOCOLATE ORANGE BREAD •

The classic combination of chocolate and orange make this bread special.

2 cups all-purpose flour
¾ cup granulated sugar
1 teaspoon baking powder
1 teaspoon baking soda
½ teaspoon salt
1 container (8 ounces) low-fat plain yogurt, at room temperature
½ cup unsalted butter, melted and cooled

2 large eggs (at room temperature), lightly beaten
1 teaspoon vanilla extract
¾ cup miniature semisweet chocolate chips
3 tablespoons finely chopped candied orange peel (see Note) or 1 teaspoon grated orange peel

1. Preheat oven to 350°F. Butter a 9 × 5 × 3–inch loaf pan. Lightly dust pan with additional flour and tap out excess.

2. In a large bowl, stir together flour, sugar, baking powder, baking soda, and salt. In another bowl, stir together yogurt, butter, eggs, and vanilla until blended. Make a well in center of flour mixture; add yogurt mixture and stir just to combine. Stir in chips and orange peel.

3. Scrape batter into prepared pan and spread evenly. Bake for 55 to 65 minutes, or until a cake tester inserted in center of bread comes out clean.

4. Remove pan to a wire rack. Cool for 10 minutes before removing bread from pan; finish cooling on rack. Store completely cooled bread in an airtight container at cool room temperature.

Makes 1 loaf; 12 to 16 slices

Note: Candied orange peel (also called glacé orange peel) is often available in gourmet food stores such as Williams-Sonoma.

• CHOCOLATE PRUNE BREAD •

Prunes add a moist, sweet flavor to a traditional chocolate loaf.

6 ounces bittersweet chocolate,
  coarsely broken
1/3 cup unsalted butter
2 cups all-purpose flour
3/4 cup granulated sugar
1 1/4 teaspoons baking soda
1/2 teaspoon salt

1/2 cup buttermilk, at room temperature
2 large eggs (at room temperature),
  lightly beaten
1 teaspoon vanilla extract
1 1/3 cups chopped pitted prunes
1/2 cup miniature semisweet chocolate
  chips

1. Preheat oven to 350°F. Butter a 9 × 5 × 3–inch loaf pan. Lightly dust with additional flour and tap out excess.

2. In a microwave-safe bowl, heat bittersweet chocolate and butter in a microwave oven on HIGH for 1 to 2 minutes, stirring halfway through cooking, until chocolate is melted. Let stand at room temperature for 10 minutes.

3. In a large bowl, stir together flour, sugar, baking soda, and salt. In another bowl, stir together chocolate mixture, buttermilk, eggs, and vanilla until blended. Make a well in center of flour mixture; add chocolate mixture and stir just to combine. Stir in prunes and chips.

4. Scrape batter into prepared pan and spread evenly. Bake for 60 to 70 minutes, or until a cake tester inserted in center of bread comes out clean.

5. Remove pan to a wire rack. Cool for 10 minutes before removing bread

from pan; finish cooling on rack. Store completely cooled bread in an airtight container at cool room temperature.

This bread freezes well.

Makes 1 loaf; 12 to 16 slices

For Chocolate Orange Prune Bread: Add 1 teaspoon grated orange peel along with the vanilla.

• COOKIES AND MILK LOAF •

A kid-pleasing recipe that's a great way to use up broken or slightly stale cookies. Try a slice with a cold glass of milk.

1¾ cups all-purpose flour
¾ cup granulated sugar
2½ teaspoons baking powder
½ teaspoon salt
1 cup milk, at room temperature
½ cup unsalted butter, melted and
   cooled

2 large eggs (at room temperature),
   lightly beaten
1½ teaspoons vanilla extract
20 cream-filled chocolate sandwich
   cookies (about 8 ounces), broken
   into small pieces (see Note)

1. Preheat oven to 350°F. Butter an 8½ × 4½ × 2¾–inch loaf pan. Lightly dust with additional flour and tap out excess.

2. In a large bowl, stir together flour, sugar, baking powder, and salt. In another bowl, stir together milk, butter, eggs, and vanilla until blended. Make a well in center of flour mixture; add milk mixture and stir just to combine. Stir in cookies.

4. Scrape batter into prepared pan and spread evenly. Bake for 65 to 75 minutes, or until a cake tester inserted in center of bread comes out clean.

5. Remove pan to a wire rack. Cool for 10 minutes before removing bread from pan; finish cooling on rack. Store completely cooled bread in an airtight container at cool room temperature.

Make 1 loaf; 10 to 14 slices

Note: Eight ounces of peanut butter cream sandwich cookies along with ½ cup semisweet chocolate chips or 8 ounces of chocolate chip cookies may be substituted for the chocolate sandwich cookies.

• CRANBERRY ORANGE OAT BREAD •

Oats add a twist to this traditional cranberry orange quick bread. To enjoy this bread year-round, buy extra cranberries in season and freeze them.

1⅓ cups all-purpose flour
½ cup uncooked, quick-cooking
*   rolled oats*
⅓ cup granulated sugar
⅓ cup firmly packed light brown
*   sugar*
2 teaspoons baking powder
½ teaspoon salt
2 large eggs (at room temperature),
*   lightly beaten*

⅓ cup milk, at room temperature
¼ cup vegetable oil
1 teaspoon vanilla extract
¾ to 1 teaspoon grated orange peel
*   (see Note)*
1 cup chopped fresh or thawed frozen
*   cranberries, drained*

1. Preheat oven to 350°F. Butter an 8½ × 4½ × 2¾–inch loaf pan. Lightly dust pan with additional flour and tap out excess.

2. In a large bowl, stir together flour, oats, sugars, baking powder, and salt. In another bowl, stir together eggs, milk, oil, vanilla, and orange peel until blended. Make a well in center of flour mixture; add egg mixture and stir just to combine. Stir in cranberries.

3. Scrape batter into prepared pan and spread evenly. Bake for 50 to 60 minutes, or until a cake tester inserted in center of bread comes out clean.

4. Remove pan to a wire rack. Cool for 10 minutes before removing bread from pan; finish cooling on rack. Store completely cooled bread in an airtight container at cool room temperature.

Makes 1 loaf; 10 to 14 slices

Note: Use 1 teaspoon grated orange peel for a stronger orange flavor.

For a lower fat, cholesterol, and sodium version: Reduce brown sugar to ¼ cup, reduce salt to ¼ teaspoon, substitute 2 egg whites for whole eggs, use ½ cup skim milk instead of ⅓ cup whole milk, and reduce oil to 1 tablespoon.

Nutrition information for lower fat, cholesterol, and sodium version per slice (¹⁄₁₄ of recipe):

102 calories
 20 grams carbohydrate
  2 grams protein
  1 gram fat
Trace cholesterol
 97 milligrams sodium

• CRANBERRY WHITE CHOCOLATE TEABREAD •

Sweet white chocolate provides a balanced counterpoint to tart, rosy cranberries.

*1 cup chopped fresh or frozen
    cranberries*
*2 tablespoons plus ½ cup
    granulated sugar, divided*
2 cups all-purpose flour
2 teaspoons baking powder
½ teaspoon salt
¾ cup milk, at room temperature

*⅓ cup unsalted butter, melted and
    cooled*
*1 large egg (at room temperature),
    lightly beaten*
1½ teaspoons vanilla extract
*6 ounces white chocolate, cut into
    ½-inch pieces*
*⅔ cup coarsely broken walnuts
    (optional)*

1. Preheat oven to 350°F. Butter an 8½ × 4½ × 2¾–inch loaf pan.

2. In a small bowl, stir together cranberries and 2 tablespoons of the sugar. In a large bowl stir together flour, remaining ½ cup of sugar, baking powder, and salt. In another bowl, stir together milk, butter, egg, and vanilla until blended.

3. Make a well in center of flour mixture; add milk mixture and stir just to combine. Stir in cranberry mixture, white chocolate, and walnuts, if desired.

4. Scrape batter into prepared pan and spread evenly. Bake for 60 to 70 minutes, or until a cake tester inserted in center of bread comes out clean.

5. Remove pan to a wire rack. Cool for 10 minutes before removing bread from pan; finish cooling on rack. Store completely cooled bread in an airtight container in refrigerator. Allow bread to reach room temperature before serving.

Makes 1 loaf; 10 to 14 slices

• FIG BREAD •

This hearty whole wheat bread is packed with figs. Try it as a nice change of pace at breakfast.

1 cup all-purpose flour
1 cup whole wheat flour
¾ cup firmly packed dark brown sugar
½ teaspoon baking soda
½ teaspoon salt
1 cup chopped, trimmed, dried Calimyrna figs

¾ cup chopped walnuts
1 cup buttermilk, at room temperature
½ cup unsalted butter, melted and cooled
1 large egg (at room temperature), lightly beaten
2 teaspoons vanilla extract

1. Preheat oven to 350°F. Butter an 8½ × 4½ × 2¾–inch loaf pan.

2. In a large bowl, stir together all but 2 tablespoons of all-purpose flour, whole wheat flour, brown sugar, baking soda, and salt. In another bowl, combine figs and walnuts with remaining 2 tablespoons of flour. (This keeps figs and walnuts from sinking to bottom of bread.) In another bowl, stir together buttermilk, butter, egg, and vanilla. Make a well in center of flour mixture; add buttermilk mixture and stir just to combine. Stir in fig and walnut mixture.

3. Scrape batter into prepared pan and spread evenly. Bake for 55 to 65 minutes, or until a cake tester inserted in center of bread comes out clean.

4. Remove pan to a wire rack. Cool for 10 minutes before removing bread

from pan; finish cooling on rack. Store completely cooled bread in an airtight container at cool room temperature.

This bread freezes well.

Makes 1 loaf; 10 to 14 slices

◆ FRESH PINEAPPLE MACADAMIA NUT ◆

Look for fresh pineapple in the salad bar section of your grocery store to save time.

2 cups all-purpose flour
1 cup granulated sugar
2 teaspoons baking powder
½ teaspoon salt
½ cup milk, at room temperature
⅓ cup unsalted butter, melted and cooled

2 large eggs (at room temperature), lightly beaten
2 teaspoons vanilla extract
1 cup chopped fresh pineapple (about ¼- to ½-inch pieces)
¾ cup chopped, salted, roasted macadamia nuts (3½-ounce jar)

1. Preheat oven to 325°F. Butter a 9 × 5 × 3–inch loaf pan.

2. In a medium-sized bowl, stir together flour, sugar, baking powder, and salt. In a medium bowl, stir together milk, butter, eggs, and vanilla until blended. Make a well in center of flour mixture; add milk mixture and stir just to combine. Stir in pineapple and nuts.

3. Scrape batter into prepared pan and spread evenly. Bake for 55 to 65 minutes, or until a cake tester inserted in center of bread comes out clean.

4. Remove pan to a wire rack. Cool for 10 minutes before removing bread from pan; finish cooling on rack. Store completely cooled bread in refrigerator. Allow bread to reach room temperature before serving.

This bread freezes well.

Makes 1 loaf; 10 to 14 slices

• HAWAIIAN LOAF •

Pineapple yogurt, macadamia nuts, dried papaya, and flaked coconut combine to create a taste of the tropics.

2 cups all-purpose flour
½ cup firmly packed light brown sugar
1 teaspoon baking powder
1 teaspoon baking soda
½ teaspoon salt
1 container (8 ounces) low-fat pineapple yogurt, at room temperature

2 large eggs (at room temperature), lightly beaten
½ cup vegetable oil
1½ teaspoons vanilla extract
½ cup chopped salted, roasted macadamia nuts
⅔ cup chopped dried papaya
⅓ cup sweetened flaked coconut

1. Preheat oven to 350°F. Butter a 9 × 5 × 3–inch loaf pan. Lightly dust with additional flour and tap out excess.

2. In a large bowl, stir together flour, brown sugar, baking powder, baking soda, and salt. In another bowl, stir together yogurt, eggs, oil, and vanilla until blended. Make a well in center of flour mixture; add yogurt mixture and stir just to combine. Stir in nuts, papaya, and coconut.

3. Scrape batter into prepared pan and spread evenly. Bake for 50 to 60 minutes, or until a cake tester inserted in center of bread comes out clean.

4. Remove pan to a wire rack. Cool for 10 minutes before removing bread

from pan; finish cooling on rack. Store completely cooled bread in an airtight container at cool room temperature.

This bread freezes well.

Makes 1 loaf; 12 to 16 slices

• LEMON BLUEBERRY BREAD •

It's difficult to resist blueberries when they are at their peak, but don't hesitate to capture the taste of summer all year long by using frozen blueberries.

BREAD

2 cups all-purpose flour
1½ teaspoons baking powder
½ teaspoon baking soda
½ teaspoon salt
1 container (8 ounces) lemon yogurt, at room temperature
1 teaspoon vanilla extract

1 teaspoon grated lemon peel
½ cup unsalted butter, at room temperature
1 cup granulated sugar
2 large eggs, at room temperature
1½ cups fresh or frozen unsweetened blueberries

LEMON DRIZZLE (OPTIONAL)

3 to 4 tablespoons sifted confectioners' sugar

1 teaspoon freshly squeezed lemon juice

1. Preheat oven to 350°F. Butter a 9 × 5 × 3–inch loaf pan.
2. *To prepare bread:* In a medium-sized bowl, stir together flour, baking powder, baking soda, and salt. In a small bowl, stir together yogurt, vanilla, and lemon peel, until blended.
3. In a large bowl, and using a hand-held electric mixer, cream together butter and sugar until blended. One at a time, add eggs, beating well after

each addition. In three additions each, alternately beat in flour mixture and yogurt mixture, beating just until combined. Stir in blueberries.

4. Scrape batter into prepared pan and spread evenly. Bake for 55 to 65 minutes, or until a cake tester inserted in center of bread comes out clean.

5. Remove pan to a wire rack. Cool for 10 minutes before removing bread from pan; finish cooling on rack.

6. *To prepare lemon drizzle:* In a small bowl, stir together 3 tablespoons of confectioners' sugar and lemon juice. Add more confectioners' sugar, if necessary, so that mixture is thick enough for drizzling. Drizzle mixture over the top of the loaf. Store completely cooled bread in an airtight container at cool room temperature.

Makes 1 loaf; 12 to 16 slices

• LEMON CRUNCH BREAD •

Cereal adds crunch to a traditional crumb topping. Our tart lemon bread is baked in a square rather than a loaf pan to maximize the amount of topping on each piece.

CRUNCH TOPPING

½ cup all-purpose flour
¼ cup firmly packed light brown sugar
⅛ teaspoon ground cinnamon

Generous dash salt
¼ cup unsalted butter, chilled
⅓ cup wheat and barley cereal (such as Grape-Nuts)

LEMON BREAD

2 cups all-purpose flour
⅔ cup granulated sugar
1 teaspoon baking powder
1 teaspoon baking soda
½ teaspoon salt
1 container (8 ounces) low-fat lemon yogurt, at room temperature

2 large eggs (at room temperature), lightly beaten
⅓ cup unsalted butter, melted and cooled
1 teaspoon vanilla extract
¾ teaspoon grated lemon peel
1 tablespoon confectioners' sugar (optional)

1. Preheat oven to 350°F. Butter a 9-inch-square baking pan. Lightly dust pan with additional flour and tap out excess.

2. *To prepare crunch topping:* In a small bowl, stir together flour, brown sugar, cinnamon, and salt. Cut butter into ½-inch cubes and distribute them over flour mixture. With a pastry blender or two knives used scissors fashion, cut in butter until mixture resembles very coarse crumbs. Stir in cereal. Set aside.

3. *To prepare bread:* In a large bowl, stir together flour, sugar, baking powder, baking soda, and salt. In another bowl, stir together yogurt, eggs, butter, vanilla, and lemon peel until blended. Make a well in center of flour mixture; add yogurt mixture and stir just to combine.

4. Scrape batter into prepared pan and spread evenly. Sprinkle topping evenly over batter to cover. Bake for 35 to 45 minutes, or until a cake tester inserted in center of bread comes out clean.

5. Remove pan to a wire rack. Cool completely. Run a knife around edges of bread to loosen sides from the pan. Invert bread onto a plate and invert again. Or serve bread from pan. Sift confectioners' sugar over top, if desired. Store completely cooled bread in an airtight container at cool room temperature.

Makes 12 servings

• MANGO APRICOT NUT BREAD •

Apricot enhances the flavor of the mango, while macadamia nuts add crunch to this rich tea loaf.

2 cups all-purpose flour
2½ teaspoons baking powder
½ teaspoon salt
½ cup granulated sugar
½ cup firmly packed light brown sugar
½ cup unsalted butter, at room temperature

2 large eggs, at room temperature
2 tablespoons milk
1½ teaspoons vanilla extract
1½ cups diced, peeled mango (see Note)
½ cup chopped salted, roasted macadamia nuts
⅓ cup finely chopped dried apricots

1. Preheat oven to 350°F. Butter a 9 × 5 × 3–inch loaf pan. Lightly dust with additional flour and tap out excess.

2. In a small bowl, stir together flour, baking powder, and salt. In a large bowl, and using a hand-held electric mixer, cream together sugars and butter for 2 minutes, or until light. One at a time, add eggs, beating well after each addition. Beat in milk and vanilla until blended. Stir in flour mixture just to combine. Stir in mango, nuts, and apricots.

3. Scrape batter into prepared pan and spread evenly. Bake for 55 to 65 minutes, or until a cake tester inserted in center of bread comes out clean.

4. Remove pan to a wire rack. Cool for 10 minutes before removing bread from pan; finish cooling on rack. Store completely cooled bread in an air-

tight container in refrigerator. Let bread reach room temperature before serving.

Makes 1 loaf; 12 to 16 slices

Note: It takes 1½ to 2 mangoes (approximately 12 ounces each) to get 1½ cups diced mango. Depending on texture of fruit (which can be quite fibrous), diced mango may look more like mashed mango.

• MARBLED PEANUT BUTTER AND CHOCOLATE LOAF •

Swirls of chocolate and peanut butter batters create this satisfying loaf. Serve it with ice-cold milk for an after-school (or work!) snack that is sure to please kids of all ages.

1 ounce semisweet chocolate
1 ounce unsweetened chocolate
2 cups all-purpose flour
2 teaspoons baking powder
½ teaspoon salt
½ cup milk, at room temperature

1 tablespoon vanilla extract
¾ cup smooth peanut butter
3 tablespoons unsalted butter, at room temperature
1½ cups granulated sugar
3 large eggs, at room temperature

1. Preheat oven to 350°F. Butter a 9 × 5 × 3–inch loaf pan.

2. In a microwave-safe bowl, heat chocolates in a microwave oven on HIGH for 1 to 2 minutes, stirring halfway through cooking, until chocolate is melted. Let stand at room temperature for 10 minutes.

3. In a medium-sized bowl, stir together flour, baking powder, and salt. In a small bowl, stir together milk and vanilla until blended. In a large bowl, and using a hand-held electric mixer, cream together peanut butter, butter, and sugar until blended. One at a time, add eggs, beating well after each addition. In three additions each, alternately beat in flour mixture and milk mixture, beating just until combined.

4. Scrape 1½ cups of batter into a medium-sized bowl and stir in melted chocolate until blended. Using a large spoon, drop alternate spoonfuls of

peanut butter batter and chocolate batter into prepared pan. Using a knife, pull it through batter in a zigzag pattern to create a marbleized pattern. Be careful not to marbleize batter too much or it will turn gray. Bake for 65 to 75 minutes, or until a cake tester inserted in center of bread comes out clean.

5. Remove pan to a wire rack. Cool for 10 minutes before removing bread from pan; finish cooling on rack. Store completely cooled bread in an airtight container at cool room temperature.

Makes 1 loaf; 12 to 16 slices

• MINI PEANUT BUTTER
CHOCOLATE CHIP BREADS •

Peanut butter and milk chocolate chips make these moist loaves reminiscent of a popular chocolate bar. Tie each with a bow as a festive Christmas treat.

1⅔ cups all-purpose flour
⅔ cup granulated sugar
1 tablespoon baking powder
¼ teaspoon salt
*½ cup smooth or chunky peanut
  butter*

*⅓ cup unsalted butter, melted and
  cooled*
¾ cup milk, at room temperature
*1 large egg (at room temperature),
  lightly beaten*
2 teaspoons vanilla extract
1 cup milk chocolate chips

1. Preheat oven to 375°F. Butter six 4½ × 2½ × 1½–inch loaf pans.
2. In a large bowl, stir together flour, sugar, baking powder, and salt. In another bowl, whisk together peanut butter and butter until smooth. Whisk in milk, egg, and vanilla until blended. Make a well in center of flour mixture; add milk mixture and stir just to combine. Stir in chocolate chips.
3. Spoon batter into prepared pans and spread evenly. Bake for 25 to 30 minutes, or until a cake tester inserted in center of one bread comes out clean.
4. Remove pans to a wire rack. Cool for 10 minutes before removing breads from pans; finish cooling on rack. Store completely cooled loaves in an airtight container at cool room temperature.

These breads freeze well.

Makes 6 loaves; 6 servings

✦ MIX-IN-THE-PAN CHOCOLATE CHIP
SNACK LOAF ✦

You can make this sweet chocolaty bread in a flash because it is mixed in the pan it is baked in! Serve with a thin layer of Chocolate Peanut Butter (see page 126).

1¾ cups all-purpose flour
¾ cup granulated sugar
⅓ cup unsweetened nonalkalized cocoa powder
2 teaspoons baking powder
½ teaspoon salt
¾ cup milk, at room temperature

⅔ cup vegetable oil
2 large eggs, at room temperature
2 teaspoons vanilla extract
1 cup miniature semisweet chocolate chips
1 tablespoon (or less) confectioners' sugar (optional)

1. Preheat oven to 350°F.

2. In an 8½ × 4½ × 2¾-inch loaf pan, stir together flour, granulated sugar, cocoa powder, baking powder, and salt.

3. Make a slight indentation in flour mixture. Add milk, oil, eggs, and vanilla. Using a fork, mix liquid ingredients slightly to combine and to break up egg yolk. Stir everything together until thoroughly combined, making sure there are no bits of flour remaining in corners or around edge of pan. Smooth surface of batter.

4. Bake for 55 to 65 minutes, or until a cake tester inserted in center of bread comes out clean.

5. Remove pan to a wire rack. Cool for 10 minutes before removing bread

56065

from pan; finish cooling on rack. Lightly sift confectioners' sugar over the top, if desired. Store completely cooled bread in an airtight container at cool room temperature.

Makes 1 loaf; 10 to 14 slices

• OAT DATE BREAD •

Oats and dates add fiber to this hearty loaf. Try it with Spiced Yogurt Cheese (page 136).

1½ cups all-purpose flour
1 cup uncooked old-fashioned rolled oats
2 teaspoons baking powder
½ teaspoon baking soda
¼ teaspoon salt
1 cup chopped pitted dates

¾ cup coarsely broken walnuts
¾ cup buttermilk, at room temperature
2 teaspoons vanilla extract
½ cup unsalted butter, at room temperature
¾ cup firmly packed brown sugar
2 large eggs, at room temperature

1. Preheat oven to 325°F. Butter an 8½ × 4½ × 2¾–inch loaf pan.
2. In a medium-sized bowl, stir together all but 2 tablespoons of flour, plus the oats, baking powder, baking soda, and salt. In another bowl, combine dates and walnuts with remaining 2 tablespoons of flour. (This keeps dates and walnuts from sinking to bottom of bread.) In a small bowl, stir together buttermilk and vanilla until blended.
3. In a large bowl, and using a hand-held electric mixer, cream together butter and brown sugar until blended. One at a time, add eggs, beating well after each addition. In three additions each, alternately beat in flour mixture and buttermilk mixture, just until combined. Stir in date and nut mixture.
4. Scrape batter into prepared pan and spread evenly. Bake for 60 to 70 minutes, or until a cake tester inserted in center of bread comes out clean.
5. Remove pan to a wire rack. Cool for 10 minutes before removing bread

from pan; finish cooling on rack. Store completely cooled bread in an airtight container at cool room temperature.

Makes 1 loaf; 10 to 14 slices

◆ PEAR PECAN LOAF ◆

This fresh fruit bread can be enjoyed year-round.

2 cups all-purpose flour
2½ teaspoons baking powder
½ teaspoon salt
1 teaspoon ground cinnamon
½ cup granulated sugar
½ cup firmly packed light brown
   sugar
½ cup unsalted butter, at room
   temperature

2 large eggs, at room temperature
2 tablespoons milk
1½ teaspoons vanilla extract
1¾ cups diced, peeled pears
½ cup chopped pitted dates
½ cup chopped pecans

1. Preheat oven to 350°F. Butter a 9 × 5 × 3–inch loaf pan. Lightly dust with additional flour and tap out excess.

2. In a small bowl, stir together flour, baking powder, salt, and cinnamon. In a large bowl, and using a hand-held electric mixer, cream together sugars and butter for 1½ minutes, or until light. One at a time, add eggs, beating well after each addition. Beat in milk and vanilla until blended. Stir in flour mixture just to combine. The batter will be stiff. Stir in pears, dates, and pecans.

3. Scrape batter into prepared pan and spread evenly. Bake for 60 to 70 minutes, or until a cake tester inserted in center of bread comes out clean.

4. Remove pan to a wire rack. Cool for 10 minutes before removing bread

from pan; finish cooling on rack. Store completely cooled bread in an airtight container in refrigerator. Let bread reach room temperature before serving.

Makes 1 loaf; 12 to 16 slices

• PLUM ALMOND QUICK BREAD •

Great for when plums are at their peak in the summer.

2 cups all-purpose flour
1½ teaspoons baking powder
½ teaspoon baking soda
½ teaspoon salt
½ cup plain yogurt, at room temperature
1 teaspoon vanilla extract
¼ teaspoon almond extract

½ cup unsalted butter, at room temperature
1 cup granulated sugar
2 large eggs, at room temperature
1 cup chopped fresh plums (about ¼- to ½-inch pieces)
¾ cup chopped almonds

1. Preheat oven to 325°F. Butter an 8½ × 4½ × 2¾–inch loaf pan.

2. In a medium-sized bowl, stir together flour, baking powder, baking soda, and salt. In a small bowl, stir together yogurt and vanilla and almond extracts until blended.

3. In a large bowl, and using a hand-held electric mixer, cream together butter and sugar until blended. One at a time, add eggs, beating well after each addition. In three additions each, alternately beat in flour mixture and yogurt mixture, beating well after each addition. Stir in plums and almonds.

4. Scrape batter into prepared pan and spread evenly. Bake for 60 to 70 minutes, or until a cake tester inserted in center of bread comes out clean.

5. Remove pan to wire rack. Cool for 10 minutes before removing bread from pan; finish cooling on rack. Store completely cooled bread in an airtight

container in refrigerator. Allow bread to reach room temperature before serving.

Makes 1 loaf; 10 to 14 slices

• POPPY SEED TEABREAD •

This easy bread can be put together in a flash. Add a little grated orange peel or lemon peel for a touch of citrus.

2 cups all-purpose flour
1 cup granulated sugar
¼ cup poppy seeds
1½ teaspoons baking powder
¼ teaspoon baking soda
½ teaspoon salt

¾ cup buttermilk, at room temperature
2 large eggs (at room temperature), lightly beaten
⅓ cup unsalted butter, melted and cooled
1½ teaspoons vanilla extract

1. Preheat oven to 350°F. Butter an 8½ × 4½ × 2¾–inch loaf pan.

2. In a medium-sized bowl, stir together flour, sugar, poppy seeds, baking powder, baking soda, and salt. In another bowl, stir together buttermilk, eggs, butter, and vanilla until blended. Make a well in center of flour mixture; add buttermilk mixture and stir just to combine.

3. Scrape batter into prepared pan and spread evenly. Bake for 45 to 55 minutes, or until a cake tester inserted in center of bread comes out clean.

4. Remove pan to a wire rack. Cool for 10 minutes before removing bread from pan; finish cooling on rack. Store completely cooled bread in an airtight container at room temperature.

This bread freezes well.

Makes 1 loaf; 10 to 14 slices

• PUMPKIN DATE QUICK BREAD •

Pumpkin makes this bread exceptionally moist. Make two loaves to use up a whole 16-ounce can of pumpkin. You could use raisins instead of dates.

1¼ cups chopped, pitted dates
3 tablespoons dark rum (optional)
2 cups all-purpose flour
1¼ cups granulated sugar
2 teaspoons baking powder
½ teaspoon baking soda
¾ teaspoon salt
1¼ teaspoons ground cinnamon

¼ teaspoon ground ginger
¼ teaspoon ground cloves
Dash ground nutmeg
1 cup canned pumpkin
2 large eggs, at room temperature
½ cup vegetable oil
⅓ cup buttermilk, at room temperature
2 teaspoons vanilla extract

1. Preheat oven to 350°F. Butter a 9 × 5 × 3–inch loaf pan.
2. In a medium-sized bowl, stir together dates and rum, if used.
3. In a large bowl, stir together flour, sugar, baking powder, baking soda, salt, and spices. In a medium-sized bowl, stir together pumpkin, eggs, oil, buttermilk, and vanilla until blended. Make a well in center of flour mixture; add pumpkin mixture and stir just to combine. Stir in date mixture.
4. Scrape batter into prepared pan and spread evenly. Bake for 65 to 75 minutes, or until a cake tester inserted in center of bread comes out clean.
4. Remove pan to a wire rack. Cool for 10 minutes before removing bread from pan; finish cooling on rack. Store completely cooled bread in airtight

container in refrigerator. Allow bread to reach room temperature before serving.

This bread freezes well.

Makes 1 loaf; 10 to 14 slices

• RHUBARB RAISIN BREAD •

Tart rhubarb adds zest and moisture to this seasonal teabread.

2 cups all-purpose flour
2 teaspoons baking powder
1/4 teaspoon baking soda
1/2 teaspoon salt
1 teaspoon ground cinnamon
1/8 teaspoon ground nutmeg
1 cup granulated sugar

1/2 cup unsalted butter, at room
   temperature
2 large eggs, at room temperature
1 1/2 teaspoons vanilla extract
1 1/2 cups diced rhubarb
1/2 cup raisins
1/2 cup chopped pecans

1. Preheat oven to 350°F. Butter a 9 × 5 × 3–inch loaf pan. Lightly dust with additional flour and tap out excess.

2. In a small bowl, stir together flour, baking powder, baking soda, salt, and spices. In a large bowl, and using a hand-held electric mixer, cream together sugar and butter for 2 minutes, or until light. One at a time, add eggs, beating well after each addition. Beat in vanilla until blended. Stir in flour mixture just to combine. Stir in rhubarb, raisins, and pecans.

3. Scrape batter into prepared pan and spread evenly. The batter will be stiff. Bake for 55 to 65 minutes, or until a cake tester inserted in center of bread comes out clean.

4. Remove pan to a wire rack. Cool for 10 minutes before removing bread from pan; finish cooling on rack. Store completely cooled bread in an airtight container in refrigerator. Allow bread to reach room temperature before serving.

This bread freezes well.

Makes 1 loaf; 12 to 16 slices

• SPICED APPLE RAISIN WALNUT TEABREAD •

This appealing round cake is moist and flavorful and is well suited for any time of day. Try it for breakfast, tuck a substantial wedge in a lunch box, or serve it along with a big pot of tea for a cozy get-together on the porch.

2½ cups all-purpose flour
1 teaspoon baking powder
1 teaspoon baking soda
½ teaspoon salt
½ teaspoon ground cinnamon
⅛ teaspoon ground ginger
⅛ teaspoon ground cloves
⅛ teaspoon ground nutmeg
½ cup buttermilk, at room temperature
1 tablespoon vanilla extract

1 cup unsalted butter, at room temperature
1½ cups granulated sugar
3 large eggs, at room temperature
2 cups loosely packed shredded, pared tart green apple
1 cup raisins
¾ cup coarsely broken walnuts
1 tablespoon (or less) confectioners' sugar (optional)

1. Preheat oven to 350°F. Butter bottom, side, and center tube of a 10 × 4–inch round tube pan. Lightly dust pan with additional flour and tap out excess.

2. In a medium bowl, stir together flour, baking powder, baking soda, salt, and spices. In another bowl, stir together buttermilk and vanilla until blended.

3. In a large bowl, and using a hand-held electric mixer, cream together butter and sugar until blended. One at a time, add eggs, beating well after

each addition. In three additions each, alternately beat in flour mixture and buttermilk mixture, beating just until combined. Stir in apple, raisins, and walnuts.

4. Scrape batter into prepared pan and spread evenly. Bake for 80 to 90 minutes, or until a cake tester inserted in center of the bread comes out clean.

5. Remove pan to a wire rack. Cool for 20 minutes before removing bread from pan; finish cooling on rack. Dust with confectioners' sugar, if desired. Store completely cooled bread in an airtight container in refrigerator. Allow bread to reach room temperature before serving.

This cake freezes well.

Makes one 10-inch round teabread; 12 to 15 slices

• SPICED PEACH BREAD •

A special summertime treat.

2 cups all-purpose flour
2¼ teaspoons baking powder
½ teaspoon salt
1 teaspoon ground cinnamon
⅛ teaspoon ground mace
1 cup granulated sugar
½ cup unsalted butter, at room
    temperature

2 large eggs, at room temperature
1½ teaspoons vanilla extract
2 cups diced, peeled peaches (see
    Note)
½ cup chopped toasted, slivered
    almonds (see Note)

1. Preheat oven to 350°F. Butter a 9 × 5 × 3–inch loaf pan. Lightly dust with additional flour and tap out excess.

2. In a small bowl, stir together flour, baking powder, salt, and spices. In a large bowl, and using a hand-held electric mixer, cream together sugar and butter for 2 minutes, or until light. One at a time, add eggs, beating well after each addition. Beat in vanilla until blended. Stir in flour mixture just to combine. Stir in peaches and almonds.

3. Scrape batter into prepared pan and spread evenly. Bake for 55 to 65 minutes, or until a cake tester inserted in center of bread comes out clean.

4. Remove pan to a wire rack. Cool for 10 minutes before removing bread from pan; finish cooling on rack. Store completely cooled bread in an airtight container in refrigerator. Allow bread to reach room temperature before serving.

Makes 1 loaf; 12 to 16 slices

Note: To remove peach skins, dip peaches into boiling water for 30 seconds and then into ice water. Peel off skin with a small paring knife.

To toast almonds, place them in a single layer on a baking sheet and bake at 350°F. for 5 to 7 minutes, shaking sheet a couple of times, until nuts are lightly browned.

• STREUSEL-TOPPED BANANA RASPBERRY BREAD •

A layer of rosy raspberry jam runs through the center of this moist banana bread. It's topped with a generous sprinkling of a spicy streusel topping. This bread would be the perfect accompaniment to any breakfast or brunch.

STREUSEL TOPPING

¼ cup all-purpose flour
3 tablespoons firmly packed brown
    sugar

¼ teaspoon ground cinnamon
2 tablespoons unsalted butter, chilled

BANANA BREAD

2 cups all-purpose flour
1½ teaspoons baking powder
¼ teaspoon baking soda
½ teaspoon salt
1 cup mashed ripe bananas (about
    2 large bananas)
⅓ cup milk, at room temperature

2 teaspoons vanilla extract
½ cup unsalted butter, at room
    temperature
¾ cup granulated sugar
2 large eggs, at room temperature
⅓ cup raspberry jam

1. Preheat oven to 350°F. Butter a 9 × 5 × 3–inch loaf pan.

2. *To prepare streusel topping:* In a small bowl, stir together flour, brown sugar, and cinnamon. Cut butter into ½-inch cubes and distribute them over

flour mixture. With a pastry blender or two knives used scissors fashion, cut in butter until mixture resembles coarse crumbs. Set aside.

3. *To prepare bread:* In a medium-sized bowl, stir together flour, baking powder, baking soda, and salt. In another bowl, stir together bananas, milk, and vanilla until blended. In a large bowl, and using a hand-held electric mixer, cream together butter and sugar until blended. One at a time, add eggs, beating well after each addition. In three additions each, alternately beat in flour mixture and banana mixture, beating just until combined.

4. Scrape half of batter into prepared pan. Carefully spread jam over surface of batter, leaving a ½-inch border around edges. Spread remaining batter over jam, smoothing surface with a spatula. Sprinkle top evenly with streusel topping. Bake for 65 to 75 minutes, or until a cake tester inserted in center of bread comes out clean.

5. Remove pan to a wire rack. Cool for 10 minutes before removing bread from pan; finish cooling on rack. Store completely cooled bread in an airtight container at cool room temperature.

Makes 1 loaf; 12 to 16 slices

• TOASTED ALMOND APRICOT LOAF •

Ground toasted almonds add crunch and flavor to this tangy bread. It's even more tempting spread with cream cheese or Apricot Butter Spread (page 123).

½ cup slivered blanched almonds, toasted (see Note)
2 cups all-purpose flour
¾ cup granulated sugar
2½ teaspoons baking powder
½ teaspoon salt
¾ cup milk, at room temperature

½ cup unsalted butter, melted and cooled
2 large eggs (at room temperature), lightly beaten
1 teaspoon vanilla extract
¾ cup finely chopped dried apricots

1. Preheat oven to 350°F. Butter an 8½ × 4½ × 2¾–inch loaf pan. Lightly dust with additional flour and tap out excess.

2. Place cooled toasted almonds in container of a food processor fitted with a steel blade; process for 15 to 20 seconds, or until very finely chopped.

3. In a large bowl, stir together chopped almonds, flour, sugar, baking powder, and salt. In another bowl, stir together milk, butter, eggs, and vanilla until blended. Make a well in center of flour mixture; add milk mixture and stir just to combine. Stir in apricots.

4. Scrape batter into prepared pan and spread evenly. Bake for 55 to 65 minutes, or until a cake tester inserted in center of bread comes out clean.

5. Remove pan to a wire rack. Cool for 10 minutes before removing bread

from pan; finish cooling on rack. Store completely cooled bread in an airtight container at cool room temperature.

Makes 1 loaf; 10 to 14 slices

Note: To toast almonds, place them in a single layer on a baking sheet and bake at 350°F. for 5 to 7 minutes, shaking sheet a couple of times, until the nuts are lightly browned.

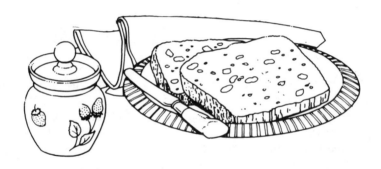

• TOASTED COCONUT BREAD •

Ground coconut provides a smooth texture with all the flavor of flaked coconut in this rich teabread.

1¼ cups sweetened flaked coconut, toasted (see Note)
⅓ cup sweetened flaked coconut
2 cups all-purpose flour
⅔ cup granulated sugar
2½ teaspoons baking powder
½ teaspoon salt

¾ cup milk, at room temperature
½ cup unsalted butter, melted and cooled
2 large eggs (at room temperature), lightly beaten
2 teaspoons vanilla extract
½ teaspoon almond extract

1. Preheat oven to 350°F. Butter an 8½ × 4½ × 2¾–inch loaf pan. Lightly dust with additional flour and tap out excess.

2. In container of a food processor fitted with a steel blade, process all the coconut until ground.

3. In a large bowl, stir together ground coconut, flour, sugar, baking powder, and salt. In another bowl, stir together milk, butter, eggs, and vanilla and almond extracts until blended. Make a well in center of flour mixture; add milk mixture and stir just to combine.

4. Scrape batter into prepared pan and spread evenly. Bake for 55 to 65 minutes, or until a cake tester inserted in center of bread comes out clean.

5. Remove pan to a wire rack. Cool for 10 minutes before removing bread from pan; finish cooling on rack. Store completely cooled bread in an airtight container at cool room temperature.

This bread freezes well.

Makes 1 loaf; 10 to 14 slices

Note: To toast coconut, spread coconut in an even layer on a baking sheet and bake at 350°F. for 4 to 7 minutes, turning coconut a couple of times, until coconut is lightly browned.

• ZUCCHINI CARROT BREAD •

The addition of zucchini and pineapple adds a twist to traditional carrot bread. This variation is great spread with cream cheese or Pineapple Orange Cheese Spread (see page 131).

1½ cups all-purpose flour
1 teaspoon baking powder
½ teaspoon baking soda
½ teaspoon salt
1 teaspoon ground cinnamon
Dash ground nutmeg
¾ cup granulated sugar

½ cup undrained, canned crushed
  pineapple packed in juice
⅓ cup vegetable oil (see Note)
2 large eggs, at room temperature
1 teaspoon vanilla extract
¾ cup shredded zucchini
¾ cup shredded carrot

1. Preheat oven to 350°F. Butter an 8½ × 4½ × 2¾–inch loaf pan. Lightly dust pan with additional flour and tap out excess.
2. In a medium-sized bowl, stir together flour, baking powder, baking soda, salt, and spices. In a large bowl, and using a hand-held electric mixer, beat together sugar, pineapple, oil, eggs, and vanilla for 2 minutes. Gradually stir in flour mixture just to combine. Stir in zucchini and carrot.
3. Scrape batter into prepared pan. Bake for 55 to 65 minutes, or until a cake tester inserted in center of bread comes out clean.
4. Remove pan to a wire rack. Cool for 10 minutes before removing bread from pan; finish cooling on rack. Store completely cooled bread in an airtight container at cool room temperature.

This bread freezes well.

Makes 1 loaf; 10 to 14 slices

Note: For a moister bread, use ½ cup vegetable oil.

For a lower fat and cholesterol version: Reduce cinnamon to ¾ teaspoon, reduce sugar to ⅔ cup, reduce oil to 2 tablespoons, use 2 egg whites instead of whole eggs, and add 1 tablespoon light corn syrup. In addition, salt may be reduced to ¼ teaspoon, if desired. Bake for 50 to 60 minutes. (The following nutrition information is based on the lower amount of salt.)

Nutrition information for lower fat, cholesterol, and sodium version per slice (1/14 of recipe):

113	calories
22	grams carbohydrate
2	grams protein
2	grams fat
0	milligrams cholesterol
100	milligrams sodium

Savory Teabreads

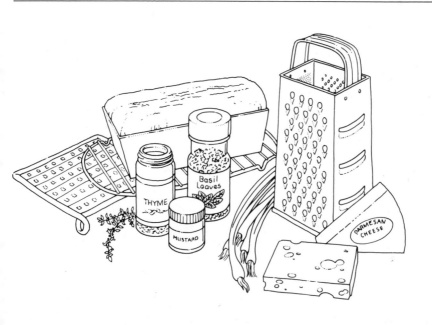

• BASIL SUN-DRIED TOMATO BREAD •

Serve this bread at your next cocktail party. Try it with Basil Garlic Butter (page 124).

2 cups all-purpose flour
1/4 cup grated Parmesan cheese
2 teaspoons dried basil leaves, crumbled
2 teaspoons baking powder
1/8 teaspoon ground black pepper

3/4 cup milk, at room temperature
1/2 cup extra virgin olive oil
2 large eggs (at room temperature), lightly beaten
3/4 cup finely chopped sun-dried oil-packed tomatoes, drained

1. Preheat oven to 350°F. Butter an 8½ × 4½ × 2¾–inch loaf pan.

3. In a medium-sized bowl, stir together flour, cheese, basil, baking powder, and pepper. In another bowl, stir together milk, oil, and eggs. Make a well in center of flour mixture; add milk mixture and stir just to combine. Stir in sun-dried tomatoes.

4. Scrape batter into prepared pan and spread evenly. Bake for 40 to 50 minutes, or until a cake tester inserted in center of bread comes out clean.

5. Remove pan to a wire rack. Cool for 10 minutes before removing bread from pan; finish cooling on rack. Store completely cooled bread in an airtight container in refrigerator. Allow bread to reach room temperature before serving.

Makes 1 loaf; 10 to 14 slices

• CHEDDAR BACON CORN BREAD •

Serve this bread warm with a hearty soup, stew, or chili.

1 cup all-purpose flour
1 cup cornmeal
2 tablespoons granulated sugar
2¼ teaspoons baking powder
¼ teaspoon salt
1 cup milk, at room temperature
2 large eggs (at room temperature), lightly beaten

3 tablespoons vegetable oil
4 drops hot pepper sauce
¾ cup shredded extra-sharp Cheddar cheese
8 slices bacon, cooked, drained, cooled, and chopped (about ½ cup)
2 tablespoons finely chopped scallions

1. Preheat oven to 350°F. Butter a 9-inch-square baking pan. Lightly dust with additional flour and tap out excess.

2. In a large bowl, stir together flour, cornmeal, sugar, baking powder, and salt. In another bowl, stir together milk, eggs, oil, and hot pepper sauce until blended. Make a well in center of flour mixture; add milk mixture and stir just to combine. Stir in cheese, bacon, and scallions.

3. Scrape batter into prepared pan and spread evenly. Bake for 20 to 30 minutes, or until a cake tester inserted in center of bread comes out clean.

4. Remove pan to a wire rack. Cool for 10 minutes before removing bread from pan; finish cooling on rack. Store completely cooled bread in an airtight container in refrigerator. Allow bread to reach room temperature before serving or toast a piece in a toaster oven for about 2 minutes, or until heated through.

Makes 12 servings

◆ CHEESY SCALLION BREAD ◆

Serve this as a savory addition to a brunch bread basket. Or cut each slice of bread into quarters and top them with a spread, such as Tapénade (page 137) as a festive appetizer.

½ cup unsalted butter
1 cup chopped scallions, including
   the tender green tops
2¾ cups all-purpose flour
1 tablespoon granulated sugar
2 teaspoons baking powder
½ teaspoon baking soda

¾ teaspoon salt
⅛ teaspoon ground black pepper
1½ cups buttermilk, at room
   temperature
2 large eggs, at room temperature
1½ cups shredded Cheddar cheese

1. Preheat oven to 350°F. Butter a 9 × 5 × 3–inch loaf pan.
2. In a large skillet, melt butter over medium heat. Add scallions and cook, stirring occasionally, for 5 to 7 minutes, or until scallions are softened. Remove skillet from heat.
3. In a large bowl, stir together flour, sugar, baking powder, baking soda, salt, and pepper. In another bowl, stir together buttermilk and eggs until blended. Stir in scallion mixture. Make a well in center of flour mixture; add buttermilk mixture and stir just to combine. Stir in cheese.
4. Scrape batter into prepared pan and spread evenly. Bake for 50 to 60 minutes, or until a cake tester inserted in center of bread comes out clean.
5. Remove pan to a wire rack. Cool for 10 minutes before removing bread from pan; finish cooling on rack. Store completely cooled bread in an airtight

container in refrigerator. Allow bread to reach room temperature before serving or toast slices in a toaster oven for about 2 minutes, or until heated through.

Makes 1 loaf; 10 to 14 slices

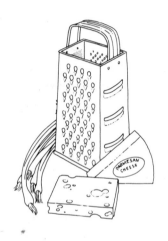

• JALAPEÑO CORN BREAD •

You can leave the jalapeño peppers out of this bread if you would like a milder teabread. Use both red and green jalapeño peppers to add a sprightly touch of color. Serve slices topped with Salsa Spread (page 135).

1 cup all-purpose flour
1 cup yellow cornmeal
1 tablespoon granulated sugar
2½ teaspoons baking powder
¾ teaspoon salt
1 cup milk, at room temperature
½ cup corn or vegetable oil
2 large eggs (at room temperature),
  lightly beaten

1½ cups shredded sharp Cheddar
  cheese
1½ cups fresh, thawed frozen, or
  drained canned corn kernels
¼ cup finely chopped jalapeño peppers
  (about 4 medium-sized peppers)

1. Preheat oven to 350°F. Butter an 8½ × 4½ × 2¾–inch loaf pan.
2. In a medium-sized bowl, stir together flour, cornmeal, sugar, baking powder, and salt. In another bowl, stir together milk, oil, and eggs until blended. Make a well in center of flour mixture; add milk mixture and stir just to combine. Stir in cheese, corn, and peppers.
3. Scrape batter into prepared pan and spread evenly. Bake for 45 to 55 minutes, or until a cake tester inserted in center of bread comes out clean.
4. Remove pan to a wire rack. Cool for 10 minutes before removing bread from pan; finish cooling on rack. Store completely cooled bread in an airtight

container in refrigerator. Allow bread to reach room temperature before serving or toast slices in a toaster oven for about 2 minutes, or until heated through.

Makes 1 loaf; 10 to 14 slices

◆ OLIVE MINI LOAVES ◆

Serve these charming small loaves next time you entertain. Place a loaf and a small container of Tapénade (page 137) at each person's seat for an inspired accompaniment to soup or salad. Experiment with some of the specialty olives that are now available. If you use olives that are especially salty, you may want to cut the salt to ¼ teaspoon.

2 cups all-purpose flour
1 tablespoon granulated sugar
2½ teaspoons baking powder
½ teaspoon salt
½ teaspoon dried thyme leaves, crumbled
¾ cup milk, at room temperature

½ cup unsalted butter, melted and cooled
1 large egg, at room temperature
Dash hot pepper sauce
1 cup chopped pitted ripe olives
1 egg yolk mixed with ½ teaspoon water for glaze

1. Preheat oven to 350°F. Butter six 4½ × 2½ × 1½–inch loaf pans.
2. In a large bowl, stir together flour, sugar, baking powder, salt, and thyme. In a medium-sized bowl, stir together milk, butter, egg, and pepper sauce. Make a well in center of flour mixture; add milk mixture and stir just to combine. Stir in olives.
3. Spoon batter into prepared pans and spread evenly. Brush egg yolk mixture over top of each loaf. Bake for 20 to 30 minutes, or until a cake tester inserted in center of one bread comes out clean.
4. Remove pans to a wire rack. Cool for 10 minutes before removing breads from pans. Serve warm. Store completely cooled loaves in an airtight

container in refrigerator. Allow bread to reach room temperature before serving.

Makes 6 loaves; 6 servings

• PARMESAN "STREUSEL" LOAF •

Add a special homemade touch to any meal with this easy-to-assemble bread. You probably have the ingredients on hand right now to make it! Spread with Roasted Red Pepper Yogurt Cheese (page 134).

PARMESAN "STREUSEL"

¾ cup grated Parmesan cheese
¼ cup all-purpose flour

3 tablespoons unsalted butter, chilled

BREAD

2 cups all-purpose flour
1 tablespoon granulated sugar
2 teaspoons baking powder
½ teaspoon salt

½ cup milk, at room temperature
½ cup unsalted butter, melted and
   cooled
2 large eggs, at room temperature

1. Preheat oven to 350°F. Butter an 8½ × 4½ × 2¾–inch loaf pan.
2. *To prepare Parmesan "streusel":* Stir together cheese and flour. Cut butter into ½-inch cubes and distribute them over flour mixture. Using your fingertips, rub in butter until mixture resembles coarse crumbs.
3. *To prepare bread:* In a large bowl, stir together flour, sugar, baking powder, and salt. In another bowl, stir together milk, butter, and eggs until blended. Make a well in center of flour mixture; add milk mixture and stir just to combine.

4. Scrape half of batter into prepared pan and spread evenly. Sprinkle surface evenly with half of the "streusel." Top with remaining batter and spread evenly. Sprinkle remaining "streusel" evenly over top. Bake for 40 to 50 minutes, or until a cake tester inserted in center of bread comes out clean.

5. Remove pan to a wire rack. Cool for 10 minutes before removing bread from pan; finish cooling on rack. Store completely cooled bread in an airtight container at cool room temperature.

Makes 1 loaf; 10 to 14 slices

• PEPPERONI CHEESE BREAD •

This bread can be made in an 8- or 9-inch-square baking pan. The 8-inch pan will make a smaller and higher bread. Either way, it's best when prepared with extra-spicy pepperoni.

1¾ cups all-purpose flour
⅓ cup whole wheat flour
1 tablespoon granulated sugar
2¼ teaspoons baking powder
¼ teaspoon salt
⅛ teaspoon dried leaf basil, crumbled

1¼ cups milk, at room temperature
2 large eggs (at room temperature), lightly beaten
¼ cup unsalted butter, melted and cooled
¾ cup shredded Swiss cheese
⅔ cup finely chopped pepperoni

1. Preheat oven to 350°F. Butter an 8- or 9-inch-square baking pan. Lightly dust with additional flour and tap out excess.

2. In a large bowl, stir together flours, sugar, baking powder, salt, and basil. In another bowl, stir together milk, eggs, and butter until blended. Make a well in center of flour mixture; add milk mixture and stir just to combine. Stir in cheese and pepperoni.

3. Scrape batter into prepared pan and spread evenly. Bake for 30 to 40 minutes, or until a cake tester inserted in center of bread comes out clean.

4. Remove pan to a wire rack. Cool for 10 minutes before removing bread from pan; finish cooling on rack. The bread is best served warm. Store completely cooled bread in an airtight container in refrigerator. To reheat, toast a piece in a toaster oven for about 2 minutes, or until heated through.

Makes 12 servings

• SAUSAGE CHEESE BREAD •

This hearty bread is the perfect accompaniment to soup.

1¾ cups all-purpose flour
⅓ cup rye flour or yellow cornmeal
1 tablespoon granulated sugar
2½ teaspoons baking powder
½ teaspoon salt
¾ cup milk, at room temperature
2 large eggs (at room temperature),
*   lightly beaten*

3 tablespoons vegetable oil
6 ounces bulk sweet Italian sausage,
*   cooked, drained, cooled, and*
*   chopped (see Note)*
¾ cup shredded provolone cheese
½ cup chopped peeled, roasted red bell
*   pepper (see Note)*

1. Preheat oven to 350°F. Butter a 9-inch-square baking pan. Lightly dust with additional flour and tap out excess.

2. In a large bowl, stir together flours (or flour and cornmeal), sugar, baking powder, and salt. In another bowl, stir together milk, eggs, and oil until blended. Make a well in center of flour mixture; add milk mixture and stir just to combine. Stir in sausage, cheese, and red pepper.

3. Scrape batter into prepared pan and spread evenly. Bake for 25 to 35 minutes, or until a cake tester inserted in center of bread comes out clean.

4. Remove pan to a wire rack. Cool for 10 minutes before removing bread from pan; finish cooling on rack. The bread is best served warm. Store completely cooled bread in an airtight container in refrigerator. To reheat, toast a piece in a toaster oven for about 2 minutes, or until heated through.

Makes 12 servings

Note: Link sausage can also be used. Simply remove casing before cooking sausage.

To roast red pepper, cut in quarters and remove seeds. Place, cut side down, on a foil-lined baking sheet. Broil for 8 to 12 minutes, or until charred. (Tops of peppers should be approximately 3 to 5 inches from the heat source.) Remove from sheet and cool. Rinse under cold running water to remove skin. Use a paring knife to remove remaining skin.

• TRICOLOR PESTO TOMATO BREAD •

A festive combination of pesto, tomato, and cheese forms the green, red, and white layers of this savory bread. Try it spread with Pesto Cream Cheese (see page 129) or Goat Cheese Spread (see page 127).

2 cups all-purpose flour
1 tablespoon granulated sugar
2¼ teaspoons baking powder
½ teaspoon salt
¾ cup milk, at room temperature
3 large eggs (at room temperature), lightly beaten

¼ cup unsalted butter, melted and cooled
¼ cup pesto sauce (see Note*)*
¼ cup grated Parmesan cheese
2 tablespoons water
3 tablespoons tomato paste

1. Preheat oven to 350°F. Butter an 8½ × 4½ × 2¾–inch loaf pan. Lightly dust with additional flour and tap out excess.

2. In a large bowl, stir together flour, sugar, baking powder, and salt. In another bowl, stir together milk, eggs, and butter until blended. Make a well in center of flour mixture; add milk mixture and stir just to combine.

3. Remove 1 cup of batter into a small bowl. Stir in pesto sauce until blended. Scrape batter into prepared pan and spread evenly with a metal spatula. Remove ¾ cup more of batter to a clean small bowl. Stir in cheese and water until combined. Scrape batter into prepared pan and spread evenly with a clean metal spatula. Stir the tomato paste into remaining batter until blended. Scrape batter into prepared pan and spread evenly with a clean

spatula. Bake for 55 to 65 minutes, or until a cake tester inserted in center of bread comes out clean.

4. Remove pan to a wire rack. Cool for 20 minutes before removing bread from pan; finish cooling on rack. Store completely cooled bread in an airtight container in refrigerator. Allow bread to reach room temperature before serving or toast slices in a toaster oven for about 2 minutes, or until heated through.

Makes 1 loaf; 10 to 14 slices

Note: Pesto sauce can be purchased fresh in many supermarkets. Or it can be prepared by using the recipe on page 130. Chunkier-style pesto sauce works best in this recipe. The bread may fall slightly and the pesto layer may be dense when using smoother pesto sauces, but the results are equally delicious.

• ZUCCHINI CHEDDAR LOAF •

Cheddar cheese and spices add zip to this savory bread that's a perfect accompaniment to dinner.

1½ cups all-purpose flour
3 tablespoons grated Parmesan cheese
1 tablespoon granulated sugar
1 teaspoon baking powder
½ teaspoon baking soda
¼ teaspoon salt
1½ teaspoons dry mustard
Generous dash ground nutmeg

Generous dash ground black pepper
2 large eggs (at room temperature), lightly beaten
⅓ cup milk, at room temperature
3 tablespoons vegetable oil
1½ teaspoons Worchestershire sauce
1 cup shredded zucchini
1 cup shredded extra-sharp Cheddar cheese

1. Preheat oven to 350°F. Butter an 8½ × 4½ × 2¾–inch loaf pan. Lightly dust with additional flour and tap out excess.

2. In a large bowl, stir together flour, Parmesan cheese, sugar, baking powder, baking soda, salt, and spices. In another bowl, stir together eggs, milk, oil, and Worchestershire sauce until blended. Make a well in center of flour mixture; add egg mixture and stir just to combine. (The batter will be very thick.) Stir in zucchini and Cheddar cheese.

3. Scrape batter into prepared pan and spread evenly. Bake for 50 to 60 minutes, or until a cake tester inserted in center of bread comes out clean.

4. Remove pan to a wire rack. Cool for 10 minutes before removing bread from pan; finish cooling on rack. The bread is best served warm. Store

completely cooled bread in an airtight container in refrigerator. Allow bread to reach room temperature before serving or toast slices in a toaster oven for 2 minutes, or until heated through.

Makes 1 loaf; 10 to 14 slices

Somewhat Healthier
Teabreads

• APPLESAUCE GINGERBREAD •

Applesauce helps keep this version of gingerbread moist—even though it's relatively low in fat. Try it plain or spread with a thin layer of Neufchâtel cheese or Plain Yogurt Cheese (see page 132).

1⅓ cups all-purpose flour
⅔ cup whole wheat flour
⅓ cup firmly packed dark brown sugar
1½ teaspoons baking powder
¾ teaspoon baking soda
¼ teaspoon salt
1 teaspoon ground ginger
¾ teaspoon ground cinnamon
⅛ teaspoon ground nutmeg

⅛ teaspoon ground cloves
⅔ cup sweetened applesauce, at room temperature
⅔ cup buttermilk, at room temperature
2 egg whites (at room temperature), lightly beaten
3 tablespoons molasses
2 tablespoons vegetable oil
½ cup raisins

1. Preheat oven to 350°F. Lightly coat an 8-inch-square baking pan with nonstick vegetable cooking spray. Lightly dust pan with additional flour and tap out excess.

2. In a medium-sized bowl, stir together flours, brown sugar, baking powder, baking soda, salt, and spices. In another bowl, stir together applesauce, buttermilk, egg whites, molasses, and oil until blended. Make a well in center of flour mixture; add applesauce mixture and stir just to combine. Stir in raisins.

3. Scrape batter into prepared pan and spread evenly. Bake for 35 to 45 minutes, or until a cake tester inserted in center of bread comes out clean.

4. Remove pan to a wire rack. Cool for 10 minutes before removing bread from pan; finish cooling on rack. Store completely cooled bread in an airtight container at cool room temperature.

This bread freezes well.

Makes 1 loaf; 12 servings

Nutrition information per serving:

155 calories
 30 grams carbohydrate
  3 grams protein
  3 grams fat
Trace cholesterol
161 milligrams sodium

• COCOA BUTTERMILK TEABREAD •

Cocoa powder is a great way to add rich chocolate flavor without a lot of fat.

1¾ cups all-purpose flour
⅔ cup granulated sugar
½ cup unsweetened nonalkalized
  cocoa powder
2 teaspoons baking powder
¼ teaspoon baking soda
¼ teaspoon salt
1¼ cups buttermilk, at room
  temperature

¼ cup vegetable oil
2 large egg whites, at room
  temperature
1½ teaspoons vanilla extract
2 teaspoons confectioners' sugar
  (optional)

1. Preheat oven to 350°F. Lightly coat an 8½ × 4½ × 2¾–inch loaf pan with nonstick vegetable cooking spray.

2. In a large bowl, stir together flour, sugar, cocoa powder, baking powder, baking soda, and salt. In another bowl, stir together buttermilk, oil, egg whites, and vanilla until blended. Make a well in center of flour mixture; add buttermilk mixture and stir just to combine.

3. Scrape batter into prepared pan and spread evenly. Bake for 50 to 60 minutes, or until bread springs back when lightly touched in center.

4. Remove loaf pan to a wire rack. Cool for 10 minutes before removing bread from pan; finish cooling on rack. Sift confectioners' sugar over top, if desired. Cool bread completely and store in an airtight container at cool room temperature.

Makes 1 loaf; 14 slices

Nutrition information per slice:

141	calories
23	grams carbohydrate
3	grams protein
5	grams fat
1	milligram cholesterol
129	milligrams sodium

• DOUBLE BRAN BREAD •

Both wheat bran and oat bran are used in this delicious high-fiber bread. Try it with Spiced Yogurt Cheese (page 136).

1 cup unprocessed bran
½ cup boiling water
1 cup all-purpose flour
½ cup oat bran
½ cup granulated sugar
1 tablespoon baking powder
½ teaspoon ground cinnamon
⅛ teaspoon salt

⅔ cup skim milk, at room temperature
¼ cup molasses
2 large egg whites, at room temperature
2 tablespoons vegetable oil
1½ teaspoons vanilla extract
½ cup currants or chopped, pitted dates

1. Preheat oven to 350°F. Lightly coat an 8½ × 4½ × 2¾–inch loaf pan with nonstick vegetable cooking spray.

2. In a medium-sized bowl, stir together unprocessed bran and boiling water and let stand for at least 2 minutes. In a large bowl, stir together flour, oat bran, sugar, baking powder, cinnamon, and salt. In another large bowl, stir together milk, molasses, egg whites, oil, and vanilla until blended. Stir in bran mixture.

3. Make a well in center of flour mixture; add milk mixture and stir just to combine. Stir in the currants or dates.

4. Scrape batter into prepared pan and spread evenly. Bake for 40 to 50 minutes, or until a cake tester inserted in center of bread comes out clean.

5. Remove pan to a wire rack. Cool for 10 minutes before removing bread

from pan; finish cooling on rack. Store completely cooled bread in an airtight container at cool room temperature.

Makes 1 loaf; 14 slices

Nutrition information per slice:

132	calories
26	grams carbohydrate
3	grams protein
2	grams fat

Trace cholesterol
105   milligrams sodium

• FRUIT AND OAT BREAD •

This moist, chewy bread is filled with fruit and flavor but is low in fat. Experiment making this bread with an assortment of dried fruits.

1 cup apple juice
1⅓ cups chopped dried fruits
    (apricots, prunes, dates, raisins)
1 cup all-purpose flour
½ cup uncooked quick-cooking
    rolled oats
⅓ cup whole wheat flour
⅓ cup firmly packed light brown
    sugar

2 teaspoons baking powder
¼ teaspoon salt
2 large egg whites (at room
    temperature), lightly beaten
1 tablespoon vegetable oil
1 teaspoon vanilla extract

1. Preheat oven to 350°F. Lightly coat an 8½ × 4½ × 2¾–inch loaf pan with nonstick vegetable cooking spray. Lightly dust pan with additional flour and tap out excess.

2. In a small saucepan, over medium heat, bring apple juice to a boil. Stir in dried fruits and remove from heat. Let stand 1 hour, or until mixture reaches room temperature.

3. In a large bowl, stir together all-purpose flour, oats, whole wheat flour, brown sugar, baking powder, and salt. In another bowl, stir together egg whites, oil, and vanilla until blended. Stir in cooled dried fruit mixture. Make a well in center of flour mixture; add dried fruit mixture and stir just to combine.

4. Scrape batter into prepared pan and spread evenly. Bake for 45 to 55 minutes, or until a cake tester inserted in center of bread comes out clear.

5. Remove pan to a wire rack. Cool for 10 minutes before removing bread from pan; finish cooling on rack. Store completely cooled bread in an airtight container at cool room temperature.

Makes 1 loaf; 14 slices

Nutrition information per slice:

129   calories
 28   grams carbohydrate
  3   grams protein
  1   gram fat
  0   milligrams cholesterol
 94   milligrams sodium

· LEMONY WHOLE WHEAT BREAD ·

This tangy tea loaf makes a terrific snack or a delicious accompaniment for salads.

1 cup whole wheat flour
1 cup all-purpose flour
½ cup granulated sugar
1 teaspoon baking powder
1 teaspoon baking soda
½ teaspoon salt
1 container (8 ounces) low-fat
  lemon yogurt (about 1 cup), at
  room temperature

2 large egg whites (at room
  temperature), lightly beaten
2 tablespoons vegetable oil
1 teaspoon vanilla extract
¾ teaspoon grated lemon peel

1. Preheat oven to 350°F. Lightly coat an 8½ × 4½ × 2¾–inch loaf pan with nonstick vegetable cooking spray. Lightly dust pan with additional flour and tap out excess.

2. In a large bowl, stir together flours, sugar, baking powder, baking soda, and salt. In another bowl, stir together yogurt, egg whites, oil, vanilla, and lemon peel until blended. Make a well in center of flour mixture; add yogurt mixture and stir just to combine.

3. Scrape batter into prepared pan and spread evenly. Bake for 40 to 50 minutes, or until a cake tester inserted in center of bread comes out clean.

4. Remove pan to a wire rack. Cool for 10 minutes before removing bread

from pan; finish cooling on rack. Store completely cooled bread in an airtight container at cool room temperature.

Makes 1 loaf; 14 slices

For Orange Whole Wheat Bread: Substitute low-fat vanilla yogurt for lemon yogurt and 1 teaspoon grated orange peel for ¾ teaspoon grated lemon peel.

Note: For a moister loaf, add 2 tablespoons of light corn syrup along with oil.

Nutrition information per slice (for lemon or orange bread):

119	calories
22	grams carbohydrate
3	grams protein
2	grams fat
1	milligram cholesterol
171	milligrams sodium

• OATMEAL RAISIN BREAD •

Reminiscent of homey cookies, this bread is perfect as a treat to tuck into a lunch box. Or serve it with a glass of milk for an after-school snack.

1 cup all-purpose flour
1 cup uncooked old-fashioned
*   rolled oats*
½ cup firmly packed brown sugar
1½ teaspoons baking powder
½ teaspoon baking soda
⅛ teaspoon salt

1 cup buttermilk, at room temperature
1 tablespoon vegetable oil
2 large egg whites, at room
*   temperature*
2 teaspoons vanilla extract
¾ cup raisins

1. Preheat oven to 350°F. Lightly coat an 8½ × 4½ × 2¾ –inch loaf pan with nonstick vegetable cooking spray.

2. In a large bowl, stir together flour, oats, brown sugar, baking powder, baking soda, and salt. In another bowl, stir together buttermilk, oil, egg whites, and vanilla until blended. Make a well in center of flour mixture; add buttermilk mixture and stir just to combine. Stir in raisins.

3. Scrape batter into prepared pan and spread evenly. Bake for 45 to 55 minutes, or until a cake tester inserted in center of bread comes out clean.

4. Remove pan to a wire rack. Cool for 10 minutes before removing bread from pan; finish cooling on rack. Store completely cooled bread in an airtight container at cool room temperature.

Makes 1 loaf; 14 slices

Nutrition information per slice:

125 calories
25 grams carbohydrate
3 grams protein
2 grams fat
1 milligram cholesterol
112 milligrams sodium

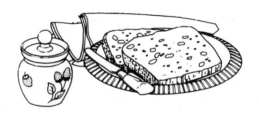

• PINEAPPLE CARROT LOAF •

Crushed pineapple in unsweetened juice keeps this loaf extra moist. This is a good choice for kids, especially if it is spread with peanut butter or Spiced Yogurt Cheese (page 136).

1 cup whole wheat flour
1 cup all-purpose flour
½ cup firmly packed brown sugar
2 teaspoons baking powder
½ teaspoon baking soda
½ teaspoon ground cinnamon
⅛ teaspoon salt
1 can (8 ounces) crushed pineapple packed in juice

2 large egg whites, at room temperature
¼ cup skim milk, at room temperature
1 tablespoon vegetable oil
1½ teaspoons vanilla extract
1½ cups shredded carrot
½ cup golden raisins

1. Preheat oven to 350°F. Lightly coat an 8½ × 4½ × 2¾–inch loaf pan with nonstick vegetable cooking spray.

2. In a large bowl, stir together flours, sugar, baking powder, baking soda, cinnamon, and salt. In another bowl, stir together pineapple, egg whites, milk, oil, and vanilla until blended. Make a well in center of flour mixture; add pineapple mixture and stir just to combine. Stir in carrot and raisins.

3. Scrape batter into prepared pan and spread evenly. Bake for 50 to 60 minutes, or until a cake tester inserted in center of bread comes out clean.

4. Remove pan to a wire rack. Cool for 10 minutes before removing bread from pan; finish cooling on rack. Store completely cooled bread in an airtight

container in refrigerator. Allow bread to reach room temperature before serving.

This bread freezes well.

Makes 1 loaf; 14 slices

Nutrition information per slice:

133   calories
 28   grams carbohydrate
  3   grams protein
  1   gram fat
Trace cholesterol
113   milligrams sodium

• STRAWBERRY BANANA BREAD •

This fruity loaf would be perfect at a summertime tea on the porch. In addition to tea (hot and iced), offer ice-cold lemonade.

1 cup chopped fresh strawberries
2 tablespoons plus ½ cup
* granulated sugar, divided*
2 cups all-purpose flour
2 teaspoons baking powder
¼ teaspoon salt
⅔ cup mashed ripe bananas (about
* 2 medium-sized bananas)*

½ cup skim milk, at room temperature
2 large egg whites, at room
* temperature*
1 tablespoon vegetable oil
2 teaspoons vanilla extract

1. Preheat oven to 350°F. Lightly coat an 8½ × 4½ × 2¾–inch loaf pan with nonstick vegetable cooking spray.

2. In a medium-sized bowl, toss strawberries with 2 tablespoons of granulated sugar.

3. In a large bowl, stir together flour, remaining ½ cup sugar, baking powder, and salt. In another bowl, stir together bananas, milk, egg whites, oil, and vanilla. Make a well in center of flour mixture; add milk mixture and stir just to combine. Stir in strawberry mixture.

4. Scrape batter into prepared pan and spread evenly. Bake for 50 to 60 minutes, or until a cake tester inserted in center of bread comes out clean.

5. Remove pan to a wire rack. Cool for 10 minutes before removing bread from pan; finish cooling on rack. Store completely cooled bread in an airtight

container in refrigerator. Allow the bread to reach room temperature before serving.

Makes 1 loaf; 14 slices

Nutrition information per slice:

127 calories
 26 grams carbohydrate
  3 grams protein
  1 gram fat
Trace cholesterol
 96 milligrams sodium

• TWO-TONE CORN BRAN BREAD •

Layers of corn bread and bran bread form a two-toned loaf that's fun to eat, yet relatively low in fat. We especially like it served warm.

BRAN BREAD

½ cup whole wheat flour
2 tablespoons granulated sugar
1 teaspoon baking powder
⅛ teaspoon salt
½ cup skim milk, at room temperature

1 egg white (at room temperature), lightly beaten
1½ tablespoons vegetable oil
1 tablespoon molasses
½ cup bran cereal (such as 100% Bran Cereal)

CORN BREAD

½ cup all-purpose flour
⅓ cup yellow cornmeal
2 tablespoons granulated sugar
1 teaspoon baking powder
⅛ teaspoon salt

½ cup skim milk, at room temperature
1 egg white (at room temperature), lightly beaten
1½ tablespoons vegetable oil

1. Preheat oven to 400°F. Lightly coat an 8-inch-square baking pan with nonstick vegetable cooking spray. Lightly dust pan with flour and tap out excess.

2. *To prepare bran bread:* In a medium-sized bowl, stir together whole

wheat flour, sugar, baking powder, and salt. In a small bowl, stir together milk, egg white, oil, and molasses until blended. Stir in bran cereal and let stand for 5 minutes. Make a well in center of flour mixture; add bran mixture and stir just to combine. Set aside.

3. *To prepare corn bread:* In a medium-sized bowl, stir together flour, cornmeal, sugar, baking powder, and salt. In a small bowl, stir together milk, egg white, and oil until blended. Make a well in center of flour mixture; add milk mixture and stir just to combine. Set aside.

4. *To assemble:* Scrape bran batter into prepared pan and spread evenly with a metal spatula. Scrape cornmeal batter into pan and spread evenly with a clean metal spatula. Bake for 15 to 25 minutes, or until a cake tester inserted in center of bread comes out clean.

5. Remove pan to a wire rack. Cool for 10 minutes before removing bread from pan; finish cooling on rack. Store completely cooled bread in an airtight container at cool room temperature.

Makes 1 loaf; 12 servings

Nutrition information per serving:

115 calories
 18 grams carbohydrate
  3 grams protein
  4 grams fat
Trace cholesterol
135 milligrams sodium

• WHOLE WHEAT IRISH SODA BREAD •

Our whole wheat version with less fat than the traditional bread is the perfect accompaniment for tea.

1 cup all-purpose flour
¾ cup whole wheat flour
¼ cup granulated sugar
1¼ teaspoons baking powder
½ teaspoon baking soda
½ teaspoon salt
½ teaspoon caraway seeds

2 tablespoons unsalted margarine or butter, chilled
⅔ cup buttermilk
2 large egg whites, lightly beaten
½ cup raisins
2 teaspoons skim milk mixed with 1 teaspoon honey for glaze (optional)

1. Preheat oven to 350°F. Lightly coat a 9-inch round baking pan with nonstick vegetable cooking spray. Lightly dust pan with additional flour and tap out excess.

2. In a large bowl, stir together flours, sugar, baking powder, baking soda, salt, and caraway seeds. Cut margarine or butter into ½-inch cubes and distribute them over flour mixture. With a pastry blender or two knives used scissors fashion, cut in margarine or butter until mixture resembles coarse crumbs. In a small bowl, stir together buttermilk and egg whites. Add buttermilk mixture to flour mixture and stir just to combine. Stir in raisins. The dough will be sticky.

3. With lightly floured hands, pat dough into prepared pan. If desired, brush some of the skim milk mixture over top of bread. With a serrated

knife, cut into 6 wedges. Bake for 20 to 30 minutes, or until a cake tester inserted in center of bread comes out clean.

4. Remove pan to a wire rack. Cool for 10 minutes before removing bread from pan; finish cooling on rack. Cut each wedge in half. This bread is best when served slightly warm. Store cooled bread in an airtight container at cool room temperature.

Makes 12 wedges

Nutrition information per wedge:

119	calories
22	grams carbohydrate
3	grams protein
2	grams fat
1	milligram cholesterol
175	milligrams sodium

Spreads

• APRICOT BUTTER SPREAD •

This tangy spread is delicious on Toasted Almond Apricot Loaf (see page 73).

4 ounces cream cheese, at room
temperature

¼ cup apricot butter

In a small bowl, stir together cream cheese and apricot butter. Serve immediately or store in an airtight container in refrigerator. Allow spread to reach room temperature before serving.

Makes approximately ⅔ cup

• BASIL GARLIC BUTTER •

Use this butter next time you make garlic bread. Spread it on sliced Italian bread, sprinkle with grated Parmesan cheese, and place it under a preheated broiler and broil until lightly browned.

½ cup unsalted butter, softened
1 to 2 tablespoons finely chopped
  fresh basil leaves

1 medium clove garlic, finely chopped

In a small bowl, stir together butter, basil, and garlic until combined. Serve immediately, or store in an airtight container in refrigerator. Allow spread to reach room temperature before serving.

Makes approximately ½ cup

◆ CHOCOLATE ORANGE CHEESE SPREAD ◆

Try this on Chocolate Prune Bread (page 34) and Chocolate Orange Bread (page 32).

2 tablespoons unsalted butter
1 ounce bittersweet chocolate
4 ounces cream cheese, at room
  temperature

⅓ cup confectioners' sugar
⅛ teaspoon grated orange peel

1. In the top of a double boiler, over hot, not simmering, water, melt butter and chocolate together, stirring often. Remove pan from heat and cool for 5 minutes.
2. In a small bowl, with a fork, beat cream cheese until smooth. Beat in sugar and orange peel. Gradually beat in chocolate mixture.
3. Cover and refrigerate until almost firm. To serve, let stand for 10 minutes at room temperature to soften. Store in an airtight container in refrigerator.

Makes approximately ¾ cup

◆ CHOCOLATE PEANUT BUTTER ◆

This is great on bagels. Try it with marshmallow cream for an exceptionally decadent sandwich!

⅓ cup heavy (whipping) cream
3 ounces semisweet chocolate,
   coarsely chopped

2 tablespoons unsalted butter
1 cup smooth peanut butter
1 teaspoon vanilla extract

   In a heavy saucepan, over medium heat, heat cream, chocolate, and butter. Remove pan from heat. Gradually stir in peanut butter and vanilla until well blended. Serve immediately or store in refrigerator until ready to serve. Allow spread to reach room temperature before serving.

Makes approximately 1½ cups

• GOAT CHEESE SPREAD •

Try this creamy spread served on Tricolor Pesto Tomato Bread (see page 94).

2 teaspoons unsalted butter
¼ teaspoon finely chopped garlic
4 ounces fresh soft goat cheese
(such as chèvre), at room
temperature

2 ounces cream cheese, at room
temperature
1 tablespoon chopped fresh basil
leaves

1. In a small skillet, melt butter over medium heat. Add garlic. Cook, stirring, for 30 seconds. Let garlic cool for 2 minutes.

2. In a small bowl, stir together cheeses, garlic butter mixture, and basil. Cover and refrigerate for several hours to blend flavors. Allow spread to reach room temperature before serving. Store in an airtight container in refrigerator.

Makes approximately ¾ cup

Variation: Omit butter and mix together ⅛ teaspoon uncooked finely chopped garlic with cheeses and basil. Proceed as above.

• HONEY MUSTARD BUTTER •

This sweet and tangy spread goes well with savory breads such as Zucchini Cheddar Loaf (page 96) or Cheddar Bacon Corn Bread (page 82).

*½ cup unsalted butter, at room
    temperature*
1 tablespoon honey
*1 tablespoon prepared spicy brown
    mustard*

1 tablespoon Dijon-style mustard
Generous dash salt or to taste

In a small bowl, stir together butter, honey, mustards, and salt. Serve immediately or store in an airtight container in refrigerator. Allow spread to reach room temperature before serving.

Makes approximately ½ cup

• PESTO CREAM CHEESE •

Serve this creamy, rich spread on savory breads such as Tricolor Pesto Tomato Bread (page 94) or use it on a sandwich of hearty whole-grain bread, sliced mozzarella cheese, and tomato.

1 package (8 ounces) cream cheese or Neufchâtel cheese, at room temperature

¼ cup pesto sauce or more to taste (see Note)

In a small bowl, stir together cream, or Neufchâtel cheese and pesto sauce until blended. Serve immediately or store in an airtight container in refrigerator. Allow spread to reach room temperature before serving.

Makes approximately 1 cup

Note: Pesto sauce can be purchased fresh in many supermarkets, or use the recipe on the following page.

• PESTO SAUCE •

This pesto sauce can be used to dress pasta as well as an ingredient in savory teabreads such as Tricolor Pesto Tomato Bread (page 94) or in spreads such as Pesto Cream Cheese (preceding page).

3 tablespoons pine nuts or walnuts
1½ cups lightly packed fresh basil leaves
½ teaspoon finely chopped garlic

Generous dash ground black pepper
⅓ cup grated Parmesan cheese
½ cup olive oil
1 teaspoon fresh lemon juice

1. In container of a food processor fitted with a steel blade, process nuts until finely ground. Scrape nuts into a small bowl.

2. Place basil, garlic, and pepper in food processor and process until finely chopped, stopping to scrape down side of the container with a rubber scraper when needed. Scrape mixture into bowl.

3. Add cheese. Stir in oil and lemon juice and stir until blended. Store in an airtight container in refrigerator. Allow sauce to reach room temperature before serving.

Makes approximately ⅞ cup

• PINEAPPLE ORANGE CHEESE SPREAD •

Try this spread on Lemony Whole Wheat or Orange Whole Wheat Bread (pages 109–10).

1 package (7½ ounces) farmer cheese
1 can (8 ounces) crushed pineapple packed in juice, drained

2 tablespoons confectioners' sugar
1 tablespoon honey
¼ teaspoon vanilla extract
¼ teaspoon grated orange peel

1. Place cheese, pineapple, sugar, honey, vanilla, and orange peel in container of a food processor fitted with a steel blade; process for 30 seconds, or until smooth, stopping to scrape down side of the container with a rubber scraper, if necessary.

2. Scrape spread into a small bowl. Cover and refrigerate for several hours to blend flavors. Allow spread to reach room temperature before serving. Store in an airtight container in refrigerator.

Makes approximately 1½ cups

◆ PLAIN YOGURT CHEESE ◆

Use this Plain Yogurt Cheese as a spread for almost any teabread, or turn it into Spiced Yogurt Cheese (page 136) as a delightful variation.

1 container (32 ounces) plain yogurt

Line a colander or strainer with cheesecloth or a clean dish towel. Place colander in the sink or over a bowl. Spoon yogurt into center of colander and gather up the edges of the cheesecloth or towel. Drain yogurt overnight or for at least 6 hours in refrigerator; the longer the yogurt drains, the firmer the finished cheese will be. Store cheese in an airtight container in refrigerator.

Makes approximately 1 cup cheese

• ROASTED RED PEPPER CHEESE SPREAD •

Serve this rich spread on Sausage Cheese Bread (page 92) or Tricolor Pesto Tomato Bread (page 94).

½ medium-sized red bell pepper,
   roasted (see page 93), seeded,
   and peeled
1 teaspoon chopped fresh basil
   leaves

¼ teaspoon finely chopped garlic
4 ounces cream cheese, at room
   temperature
2 tablespoons grated Parmesan cheese

1. Place pepper, basil, and garlic in container of a food processor fitted with a steel blade. Process until almost smooth. Add cheeses and process until well blended, stopping to scrape down side of the container with a rubber scraper if necessary.

2. Scrape spread into a small bowl. Cover and refrigerate for several hours to blend flavors. Allow spread to reach room temperature before serving. Store in an airtight container in refrigerator.

Makes approximately ¾ cup

• ROASTED RED PEPPER YOGURT CHEESE •

Great on crackers or as a dip for raw vegetables. Use drained bottled roasted red peppers or roast your own (see page 93).

1 recipe Plain Yogurt Cheese (page 132)
3 tablespoons finely chopped roasted red pepper
1½ tablespoons finely chopped scallions
Salt, to taste
Freshly ground black pepper, to taste

In a small bowl, stir together Plain Yogurt Cheese, red pepper, scallions, salt, and pepper. Store in an airtight container in refrigerator.

Makes approximately 1⅓ cups

• SALSA SPREAD •

This spread is also great with crackers as an appetizer. Use reduced-fat cream cheese and Cheddar cheese for a lower-fat spread.

½ cup chopped tomatoes
1 tub (8 ounces) cream cheese or light cream cheese, at room temperature
1 cup (4 ounces) shredded Cheddar cheese or reduced-fat Cheddar cheese

1½ tablespoons finely chopped scallions
1 tablespoon finely chopped fresh or drained, bottled jalapeño peppers
1 tablespoon finely chopped fresh coriander

1. Place chopped tomatoes on a paper towel to remove some of the liquid.
2. In a medium-sized bowl, and using a hand-held electric mixer, beat cream cheese and Cheddar cheese together until combined. Using a rubber scraper, fold in tomatoes, scallions, jalapeños, and coriander until combined. Serve immediately or store in an airtight container in refrigerator. To serve, let stand for 10 minutes at room temperature to soften.

Makes approximately 1½ cups

◆ SPICED YOGURT CHEESE ◆

This mild-flavored spread is delicious with many of the quick breads.

1 recipe Plain Yogurt Cheese
  (page 132)
1 to 2 tablespoons granulated sugar

¼ teaspoon ground cinnamon
Dash ground cloves
Dash ground nutmeg

In a small bowl, stir together Plain Yogurt Cheese, sugar, cinnamon, cloves, and nutmeg. Store in an airtight container in refrigerator.

Makes approximately 1 cup

• TAPÉNADE •

For an appealing appetizer, serve this spread with slices of potatoes. Cook small new potatoes until they are just tender. Cut the potatoes into thick slices and spread some of this flavorful French-style olive mixture on top of each one. Also serve this spread with such savory teabreads as Cheesy Scallion Bread (page 83) and Olive Mini Loaves (page 87).

1 can (about 6 ounces drained weight) pitted ripe olives, drained
1 can (2 ounces) anchovy fillets in olive oil, drained
2 tablespoons olive oil

1 tablespoon drained capers
1 tablespoon prepared spicy brown mustard
1 small clove garlic, coarsely chopped
⅛ teaspoon freshly ground black pepper

1. Place olives, anchovies, oil, capers, mustard, garlic, and pepper in container of a food processor fitted with a steel blade. Process for about 1 minute, or until combined (mixture should still have a coarse texture), scraping down side of the container with a rubber scraper if necessary.

2. Scrape spread into a small bowl. Serve immediately or cover and refrigerate to blend flavors. Store in an airtight container in refrigerator.

Makes approximately 1¼ cups

Index